HOW TO BE F*CKING AWESOME

STICKING A FINGER UP TO THE LAW OF ATTRACTION AND A THUMB UP TO ACTION

DAN MEREDITH

R∃THINK PRESS

First published in Great Britain 2016 by Rethink Press
(www.rethinkpress.com)

Front cover illustration © Jamie Alderton

DISCLAIMER

Right, before you turn a single page I want to give you a bit of a heads up.

This book is a little… er, different.

I have written this in a conversational, easy to read, don't-waste-your-time format. There may be an emoticon or two.

I start more than one sentence with 'and'.

Swearing? In real life I swear – so I also swear in this book.

So if any of the above offends you, this book may not be for you and that's totally OK! There are *thousands* of books out there that will likely be perfect for you, and I'm always happy to recommend.

On final thing: I give some more 'woo-woo' thinking and concepts a little bit of a bashing – *but* I have *lots* of friends in this world, and I love them dearly. They tolerate my beliefs, and me, and the same goes for me towards them. Just because we disagree on things doesn't mean we don't get along. Because we do.

And if that stuff works for you? Awesome. I'm just sharing what I know, from my experience, in an effort to help folks who maybe need something a little more 'tenacious' – a combination of a kick up the arse and an arm around the shoulder.

Heads up given.

You have been politely warned.

So, I guess the last thing for me to say is read this book with an open mind. I hope you find it entertaining, and you are welcome to drop me an email on dan@coffeewithdan.com if that tickles your fancy.

Good luck!

CONTENTS

INTRODUCTION

WHY THIS BOOK?

So you're probably thinking, what the hell is this book all about? To be honest I'd be wondering the same thing if I was you.

But if I told you that this book had the potential to change your life, then would you pay attention?

Of course you would.

Actually, seeing as we're already thinking and wondering about things...

Have you ever thought why some people have such an awesome life, plenty of money, amazing friends and a business they love? Yet others struggle at every step, are constantly broke and can never get out of the daily rut.

I pondered the exact same thing a couple of years ago.

I desperately wanted to get in on the 'secret of success'. I wanted to know how some people could be resilient and optimistic no matter what life threw at them, emerging ever stronger, ever fulfilled, and ever successful. While others, regardless of their talents and 'lucky as fuck' life, remained negative, bitter, and unsuccessful human beings.

And I started looking for answers.

I became an Amazon 1-click whore-bag, buying book after book in my early thirties, trying to better myself, find the 'answers' or simply give myself the kick up the arse that I needed to get my shit into action.

This book is a result of three years of quite ridiculous adventure into the world of entrepreneurism, and many, many years before that *wanting* to do it, but never having the balls to actually step up and give it a go.

This book, in my humble opinion, is the essence of the 'answers' I found from not only reading but also *implementing* the knowledge. It answers the most important question that I had at the time, and now you reading this book probably have:

'Is it really possible to be fucking awesome, live life on your own terms, make a difference and be truly fulfilled, all the while having fuck loads of F.U.N?'

Yep.

I'll show you how, in this book. Here, I've outlined eleven key 'things' that I have found from analysing my own life, and spending one-on-one time with some of the most successful people on the planet, which (I hope) will allow you to do just that. Live an epic life.

As of writing, I seem to have tens of thousands of people all round the world who like – and trust me, this weirds the fuck out of me – seem to want to know how I do what I do.

Honestly, I'm just a daft, hairy plum of a human who has somehow gone and got himself all successful.

And if you've seen what I look like, you have no excuses...

WHY YOU? WHY ME?

That's a good question. You, dear reader – I have no idea who you are, what your situation is, what makes you happy, what turns you on or simply makes you so incandescent with rage that you want to head-butt a wall (or maybe that's just me). Don't worry, though, we are coming to you in just a moment...

Anyway, I digress.

I wrote this book for me first and foremost. It's the one thing I wish I could go back in time and give to the younger Dan to tell him to stop waiting for things to happen and simply go out there and bloody *make* them happen.

If I handed this book to him, he probably wouldn't have a clue what he was doing with it. But one thing I have learned, as you will see, is that pretty much nobody does – and when you know that, it's rather liberating.

Look, we have all read those rags-to-riches books where one minute someone is living in a field, selling toenails to make ends meet, and the next they have 100 squillion (yes, that's a made up word) pounds and a golden space yacht.

Whatever.

To those people: more power to you!

However, I grew up in the West Country of the UK – lovely place to be a young chap, but everything is pretty relaxed. When I was growing up, you didn't need much to live – compared to cities anyway. You could get a normal job and have a pretty good *normal* life.

(If that is what you want, by the way, then this book may not be for you – just a heads up.)

My mum and dad both worked their arses off. I never wanted for anything, but money was tight – and I didn't realise the sacrifices they had made to provide for me and my sister until

I was older.

Now, my sister Anna wasn't blessed with the good fortune of full health like I was. She was born with Epilepsy and, unfortunately, had such a traumatic fit when she was a little one that it left her severely brain damaged.

Why am I telling you this?

Because the act of bettering yourself, growing a business, having more freedom or shit loads of pennies to play with is great – if that's your thing. But ever since I was in my early teens, I realised that if I wanted to provide for Anna (and treat my parents for being fucking amazing – I mean, I really don't know how they did and still stayed sane. Happily married, too), I was going to have to make money.

Quite a bit of it.

In fact, apart from a few material things, I don't want for much. I got the watch that meant the world to me a little while back; I like to travel; I *clearly* like to eat. But outside of that, I'm a simple creature.

So an excess of money and material things was never the goal.

I wanted to make it clear that everything I have done, put myself through and sacrificed has been for Anna and my parents. They're my 'Why'.

Now, if this was a 'normal' book, lol – and I'm completely happy in my mid-thirties using lol – this would be the bit where I am supposed to evoke an emotional response so you get more buy-in with me, love me and my story. You know, the zero to hero sorta thing...

Fuck that.

Look, I had an awesome childhood. My parents were loving, and my sister – although she will never get to experience a fraction of what I do – is still a little shit!

She is my little sister, after all, eh?

So with that out of the way, you might be wondering why I am writing this book at all. I mean, I'm OK when it comes to education (failed my A-levels first time, had to go back and do them again), hardly the most handsome man on the planet – unless you like large, bear-like humans – and I spent the majority of my twenties doing pretty well in various careers. But you know what? I never felt in any way, shape or form fulfilled.

Every single Monday morning, I would be shattered as I'd been awake until stupid o'clock because I didn't want to go to work.

I looked at the people with the freedom, the money, the lifestyle I wanted, and you know what? I fucking hated them.

I thought they had something special that I didn't have, that Mummy and Daddy had given them a bastard trust fund, or they were simply lucky.

I was fed up with people saying I had a talent; that one day I would make it; I could be 'somebody'. I felt that I was supposed to do something more with my life than sit in an office, slowly going insane, making someone else money while life slipped by me.

I didn't want to wake up in my forties, fifties, sixties or seventies, look back on my life and go: 'Ahhh, bollocks!'

So, at thirty-three, I said, 'Fuck it!'

I had simply had enough.

I had spent the majority of my life making excuses for why I hadn't achieved X or Y, instead of doing what I do now.

Look, I am in *no* way saying that I'm awesome (which is ironic considering it's the title of the book. Told you this wasn't going to be a normal book, eh?), but I am going to show you what it took for me to become 'awesome' in my own eyes.

Your awesome and my awesome may be totally different, and that's A-OK. But the plan is, by the time you have read this, you will either hate me or be fired up enough to go and *do something*! Hopefully, the eleven lessons to come will show you

– from what I have learned – what is needed to make it in this rather ridiculous world today.

And where am I right now? Ahhh, here is the bit where I give you the 'ole social proof'. You know, where I show you a picture of my fancy life, or golden space yacht, or what have you.

Nope. That's not how I roll.

But I will tell you this: back end of 2013 I had borrowed as much as I could and maxed out every single credit card I owned. I was doing monthly credit card shuffles just to pay the bills. Every day I had a choice to make: do I put fuel in the car or go to Tesco at 9.45pm and get what I can from the 'no one wants this shit and it's going off tomorrow' section?

(If I ever see Tilapia or oats again, I think I will weep…)

Now, as of writing this, I have a fully automated fitness facility (I literally do nothing; it's criminal), a very successful copywriting business, a digital agency launching, over 4,000 people in my Facebook group 'Coffee With Dan', hundreds in my membership site 'Espresso With Dan', thirty+ private clients all over the world, a stupid amount of speaking gigs lined up…

Oh, and I am just about to bring one of the world's most loved entrepreneurs – Mr Gary Vaynerchuk – to London for a sell-out event.

And three years ago, having enough money to get a pizza was a struggle.

Makes you think, eh?

Equally when you read this I may be back in that field, selling my toenails to make ends meet. Who knows what life has in store, but I'll tell you one thing: I would be *the* best toenail salesman. Ever. Times ten.

SO HOW DO YOU USE THIS BOOK?

Totally up to you. I used to get so overwhelmed by reading a whole book, it felt almost like I was back at school.

For that reason I have put this book in a 'kinda' order – an order which I think is most beneficial. But that's my brain, not yours. I don't want to overwhelm you with more info; I want you to take action. Get shit done.

I'm a simple creature by nature – and I've made this really simple. I call it my Be/Do approach. Each chapter sets out what you need to *be* in order to be fucking awesome. And it's not what most people think.

It's not having stuff, or even doing stuff. It's much simpler than that. It's making the fucking decision to do so. Decide to be awesome and everything will slot into place.

At the end of each chapter is what I believe you need to *do* to be awesome. This again is from my own experiences.

Be.

Do.

It really is that simple!

Here's a tip – have a look at the chapters. See one that interests you? Go read that. Pressed for time or lazy as balls? Then go to the end of each chapter where you'll get a summation as well as some things you can do.

If you get even one thing from this book that you can apply to your life, trust me, you have got your money's worth. But only if you take action.

Do me a favour: don't read this and get all fired up then do nothing. I mean it. That proper gets on my tits. Just commit to changing *one* thing at least after reading this book – even if it's messaging me to say you hate it, at least it's action!

Oh, and some chapters are long, some are short – just enough for you to use and implement. Put it this way: when there are lots of rules you are supposed to stick to when writing a book, I enjoy being a naughty little shit and doing things my own way!

I don't believe in you wasting your time reading words for the sake of it, and I can't be arsed to write them just for the sake of it. I decided to write this book in seven days. I wasted three of them twatting about online. I'm pushing the tolerance of human caffeine consumption to teach you this shit, so I hope you like it.

And if you don't? That's awesome too!

WHAT TYPE OF PERSON WILL GET THE MOST OUT OF THIS BOOK?

Do you feel ready to take your game to the next level? Maybe you feel like you have been at a standstill in life and business, or you're simply bored shitless and want to give this 'becoming awesome' thing a go. Well why not push the button and see what happens?

As you *may* have noticed, I am a chap – and yes, as you have seen, I do use the odd swear word. This is me. When I used to try to be someone else or hide who I am, I was nowhere near as successful as I am now. But even though I am of the male persuasion, I couldn't give two shits what is between your legs. All I care about is what is in between your ears, and what you *do* with that brilliant brain of yours!

Remember, my sister didn't have that privilege. It's a powerful fucker – don't waste it.

WHO IS THIS BOOK *NOT* FOR?

Do you believe in asking the universe to fix your problem, manifesting, vibrations or any other hippy bollocks? Do one! Lol.

That sounds harsh – and weirdly I seem to attract quite a few people in this crowd, which may sound hugely contradictory considering the above statement. But if that's what you believe in, *more power to you*! I massively respect people's beliefs, and I hope in turn you respect mine. I have just seen too many people in this space (and they are lovely, kind, caring people as a rule) really struggle.

Seriously, though, if you do practise the above and it *is* working for you – don't stop! If it's giving you the life you want, that's awesome and I want to take nothing away from that.

Me, though? I prefer *action*.

It's pretty simple, my philosophy. It's the core message of my groups, my businesses and my life in general.

What I believe in is the power of *Getting. Shit. Done.*

1

BE SELFISH

To be successful you have to be selfish, or else you never achieve. And once you get to your highest level, then you have to be unselfish. Stay reachable. Stay in touch. Don't isolate.

MICHAEL JORDAN

I wanted to kick off this book with a nice, controversial topic. If you know me, then you know I don't do convention. I speak total brutal honesty. And so fuck it, I'm going to start with some brutal truths, one of which is that, if you ever want to get anywhere in life, you've gotta start getting a little selfish.

I'm sure this will annoy a few folks. And if that's you, all I ask is that you read to the end of the chapter to let me explain why this is so important, and how you can apply it to your life without coming across as a complete prick.

What you'll learn in this chapter probably outweighs everything else in the book, as it's the first step to really owning your life. And the decisions you make.

You see, if there's anything I have learned about truly successful and awesome people it's that they were once selfish with their time. And some still are. In fact, it is that exact selfishness that got them to where they are today.

We're told as kids not to be selfish. Which is total bollocks, in my opinion.

Why?

It's gearing up our kids (well not mine, I don't have any, but you know what I mean) to think about everyone but themselves. It shows them that it's actually good to think about others and totally fucking ignore yourself, your dreams, your ambitions and your thinking.

It's the industrial age thinking: do what you are told. Work for others all your life, follow orders, take your money and shut the fuck up. Spend your life doing other people's shit and ignoring your own shit till some fucking end date (retirement) which you don't even know you'll reach.

And then you depart this world with no legacy of your own 'cause you were too busy living for others rather than making your own mark on this small planet of ours.

Not entirely a remarkable, awesome life, is it?

So read on and keep an open mind. Don't worry, you can thank me later.

Now you may be footloose and fancy free. You may be married with kids. You could be like me and have a family member or friend you help support. You may – like my good friend, and she shall remain nameless – have said 'No, thank you' to human beings in order to collect all the cats.

Whatever your situation, but especially if you support someone else, I am going to ask you to do this:

Look after #1. That's *you*.

Now I am *not* a parent (yet – er, I hope, anyway), but *many* people who I have coached, mentored and worked with over the years are. They believe they have to sacrifice everything for their offspring – much as my folks did. However, those who, even for a short period of time, focused on themselves first ended up being better partners, parents, friends – you name it.

I know this, because I used to be exactly the opposite of those people. I put everyone else first and myself last. But after a while, it got kinda tough.

What you need to realise is that, if you don't sort yourself out first, then you can't do justice to those people who rely on you or your support.

No fucker is going to do this for you. It's on your shoulders to take ownership.

You see, for so long I worked myself *stupid* (100–120 hour weeks were fairly commonplace in my life), to the point that yes I had money coming in to provide where necessary, but I ended up burned out, ill and unable to work.

Ergo, a fucking waste of time. But, all I knew was hard work.

Don't get me wrong – if you want to make it in the entrepreneurial world, business or life, you do have to fucking work, and hard at times! But the big mistake that I made was not looking after myself before sorting everyone else out.

Case in point: I had reached a six-figure income (I don't know about you, but I fucking hate that phrase) in three different industries all for the 'grand plan' of providing a safe and secure future for my sister and an epic-as-balls retirement for Mum and Dad. Oh and, you know, the odd nice thing for me from time to time.

(And pizza. Lots and lots of pizza.)

But to get there I was working harder and longer than anyone else (as well as some Jedi shit I'll tell you about later) until I ended up hating life and quitting – just to start all over again.

As I mentioned earlier, it took till I was thirty-three to basically give myself permission (more on that later) to create a business and a life *that was just for me*. As a result of removing the pressure to provide and the looming deadline of 'the future', I have been able to create multiple businesses, win back my freedom, and in the process begin to build an empire that will meet my goals.

The crazy thing is that being a little bit selfish actually makes your and everyone else's life better!

If you've ever been on an aeroplane and actually listened to the cabin crew, you'll recognise the following:

'Fit your own oxygen mask before attempting to help others fit theirs.'

You can't help others if you're dying yourself, right?

You *have* to sort yourself out before you can in any way go about helping others. Once you have all your 'ducks in a row', *then* you can go about making a difference to the people whose lives you impact.

It's all very well me stating that. Now I'm going to make it easier and break down some areas that I feel you need to really 'dial into'.

Take care of your health. Look, if you have followed me on social media or know my backstory, I'm quite open that I have had some problems with both drinking and a 'hypomanic' personality (highs and lows – I have found it actually quite beneficial now I know how to manage it).

I would deal with stress and 'the dark times' by either hitting the vodka or smashing in an obscene amount of junk food in an effort to make myself feel better. Considering I came from a rugby playing/weight lifting/personal training background, to say I fucking hated myself at points was actually quite an understatement. I mean, I was a personal trainer! I should know better than to abuse my body like that.

Plus I never spoke to *anybody* about the shit I was going through, the thoughts in my head, how I was feeling. Nothing. To all intents and purposes, I was happy as a clam and living an epic life.

All b-b-b-b-b-bullshit!

I was so focused on growing the business that I completely neglected the things that got me there in the first place.

I'm not going to tell you what to do specifically, just don't do what I did and go so far the other way that you completely forget to take care of both your body and your mind. As of writing, I'm pleased to say my health and nutrition are on point, I don't bottle shit up anymore and I actually wake up without feeling like death.

Which is nice.

I'm going to keep my advice dirty simple.

Exercise – it's not fun, especially to start with, but you need to do it. Me? I like to lift things and hit things. Do your research, find out what you like/what's going to get you the most benefit, hire a personal trainer for a few sessions (at least to get you up and running), make it a part of your life. Have it in your diary as a non-negotiable block-it-out make-it routine. End of.

Nutrition – try to eat as much 'real food' as you can. Don't believe what the media says is best for you – as a rule, if there's a best-selling book espousing a certain type of diet, it's probably a load of shite. (I am very lucky to count some of the world's best in this area as friends). Don't beat yourself up if you have a pizza or a Pinot – just don't do it all the time. Simple.

Mental health – ahhh, the elephant in the room. I have found that those of us who identify as being entrepreneurs seem (from anecdotal evidence and my group) to have a higher incidence of issues in the 'ole noggin' than most. Just going to say this – get a support network. Have people you trust around you and, if you feel down/stressed, fucking talk to them.

Equally, there is nothing wrong if you speak to a professional. Get that shit sorted. It's normal; people are just too afraid to talk about it.

Anyone doesn't like you or judges you for it? Fuck 'em – which leads me on to the next point.

Remove toxic people and places from your life. Once you do this, you will feel like a 20kg backpack has been removed from your shoulders. I'm serious. I let toxic individuals stay in my life far too long. These folks – and I don't think they are bad people per se – took up so much of my headspace that since I have removed them my work rate, happiness and bank balance have sky rocketed!

You don't have to be an arse about it. I find that simply unfollowing someone on social media or slowly distancing yourself from certain individuals who sap the energy out of you generally removes their negative ways, which normally works a treat.

If they are still causing you grief, though, block them from your life on every communication channel. They may piss and moan for a bit, but they'll soon burn out and find someone else to give shit to. When you don't hear from them anymore, they'll simply disappear from your life.

Your time is precious. Be selfish with it and don't let people steal from you what can't be brought back.

With regards to places – if you go to places where you end up doing things you regret, or simply shouldn't do, don't go there. Willpower can be a bitch, so if you don't put yourself in situations that can make bad shit happen, it simply won't.

The more you distance yourself from negativity, the more space it leaves for positive people to flow into your life.

You time! Ahhh, this is where we get to the bit that sounds odd, but once you have got used to it, it makes life so much better.

I'll go into more detail in a later chapter how to program this into your life, but you need to make sure – especially if you have dependents – that you do this.

In the hustle of modern life, trying to grow a business, and make changes, it's all too easy to let things slip. And once they are gone, it's a right bugger to get them back.

Now this can be anything. As a rule I like a mix of family time (with kids, parents, etc.), date time (if you have a partner), dumb shit (stuff you like doing just for the sake of it), entertainment (films, books, museums, day trips, nights out, dinners, etc.) and nothing time.

All the above are important, and they are important every week. Again I'll show you how to schedule them later; now I'm trying to hammer home that you still have to be you! You are not defined by your commitments. You owe it to yourself to be the person your friends and family love and enjoyed spending time with *before* you embarked on growing your business, making drastic life changes, or whatever goal you have set yourself.

I lost someone I cared very much for because I put work above *everything* else, and I know many people who have the same regrets. Don't make the mistakes I did – learn from them. Don't stop being you, and you do that by making *time* to be you.

This may sound a little throwaway but it is really important shit, hence I kicked the book off with this chapter.

Equally, I want you to consider what 'being awesome' means to you. How much do you want to achieve the next level in your business and life? Do you wake up thinking about it every day? Is it something you will get round to someday, just not right now? Does it fill you with a burning rage that you haven't achieved all that you desire yet?

You are going to have to get used to being selfish to the level you want to achieve your goals in life.

I'm going to say something that seems contradictory to what I've seen in quite a few motivational and self-help books: you *can't* have it all.

Well, not right away, anyway.

This book is a little different as I'm selling things that are unsexy – hard work and sacrifice. I know there are people (you can find these absolute nuggets online. Shouldn't be hard – they will be telling you how easy life is. Every. Fucking. Day) who say you can have it all without any sacrifice at first.

Bullshit.

They often forget to mention how hard they worked to get to the point where they have it all. They give you the zero to hero story but fucking miss out the 'difficult-fucking-road-they-had-to-go-through-but-don't-mention-'cause-it-aint-sexy-enough'.

Yeah. That.

Hard work and sacrifice don't sell, so they are probably dumb ideas for a book. But, like I said earlier, I don't give a shit if this sells ten or 10,000 copies – I'm writing it for me. And if people get value from it, sweet.

Unfortunately, I have been burned with false promises before and, dear reader, I don't want you to think this is going to be a walk in the park.

You are going to have to be selfish.

You are going to have to make sacrifices.

There is no way around it.

If you are happy where you are in life right now, then keep doing what you're doing. But if there is something gnawing away at you inside, and you always feel that there is more to life, then evaluate what you are going to hang on to, and what you are willing to sacrifice for a period of time.

Oh, and how long is that period of time? As a guestimate from my own experience – minimum of two years' relentless work, assuming you have the required skills for what you are trying to do to make it to some degree or other.

Told you I can't sell that shit.

Finally, another thing I want you to get over, if you have an issue with this, is rewarding yourself. If you are going to work your arse off, be selfish, make sacrifices – when you hit a milestone, smash a goal or simply achieve something that you thought impossible, reward yourself.

I don't know if it's a British thing or what, but we seem to struggle to recognise and reward success, and reluctant to treat ourselves. Well, if you have worked for it, earned it, made it happen, you *deserve* to treat yourself to something you want!

It could be a new home, a tropical holiday, a new car, some fancy shoes – totally up to you. But what is the point in all that hard work if you don't treat yourself from time to time? It's not *always* about others. You are the one doing the work, after all.

As I said in the introduction, I am actually pretty simple and don't have crazy expensive tastes, but I have always loved a good watch. When I was thirteen or fourteen, I remember being with my dad and he showed me a Rolex Submariner. He said to me that when I was grown up, if I could walk into the shop and pay for it – cash – I could say (in his eyes) I had 'made it'.

Fast forward twenty-three years and I did exactly that. I bought the blue and gold Rolex I had wanted ever since then. Is it a bit flash?

Of course it is!

But did I work for it? Well flying over 50,000 miles, sixty+ train trips, investing every penny I made back into training, masterminds and coaching, working sixteen–eighteen hour days as the norm (sometimes twenty-four hour+ bad boys) and hammering my health and sanity in the process…

Yeah, I worked for it.

So when you do hit a big goal or milestone, be selfish. Do something for *you*. Because without you, nothing else happens.

BE SELFISH TO DO/ACTION STEPS

Take ownership and look after yourself *first*. Now look, no fucker is going to do this for you. It's all on your shoulders. If you're dying yourself, you can't help anyone else. To be the success you want to be, you're going to have to start fitting your own oxygen mask before attempting to help others. Your exercise, nutrition and mental health come first. Block times in your diary that are non-negotiable and make them routine.

Remove toxic people and places from your life. The more you distance yourself from negativity, the more space it leaves for positive people and experiences to flow naturally into your life. This doesn't mean you have to do anything drastic – it could be something as simple as blocking negative people on Facebook.

Consider what 'being awesome' means to you. If you want to achieve the next level in business and life, you're going to need to go balls deep on this. Ask the uncomfortable questions to bring out the truth. What is it you wake up every day thinking about?

Reward yourself. This doesn't need much explanation or many action steps. You work your arse off in work, you make sacrifices, so when you smash a milestone and achieve something that you didn't think was possible, reward yourself. You *deserve* to treat yourself to something you want, you know!

2

BE SHAMELESS
(YOU'RE A LONG TIME DEAD)

It's kind of fun to do the impossible.
WALT DISNEY

Ahh, the art of being shameless. And it is an *art*, 'cause it's bloody fun as fuck when you start doing it.

Why?

Well, when you truly become shameless, you reach a new height of freedom – the freedom of not giving two hoots what people think about you. And that's liberating, to say the least.

You'll learn in this chapter how ego and pride can fuck you up, so the sooner you get rid of them, the more awesome you'll become.

You need to become shameless in all aspects of your life, whether that's learning new skills, business or your health and relationships.

Remember the time you didn't approach that good-looking bombshell (or insert ladies' equivalent. They probably have abs or something) because you were scared you'd make a fool of yourself? And then later you realised that she was actually into geeky nerds and ended up marrying a bigger nerd than you!

Burnnnn!

What I mean is that the more you care about what people might say, do, or how they'll treat you, the more miserable you become.

Before you read the rest of this chapter, for one minute just imagine how your life would have been if you'd done more of the things you wanted to do but were too scared. That job you wanted but felt you weren't qualified enough. That event you wanted to go to but didn't because your friends would have laughed at you. Or even the life you wanted to live, but haven't done so because it's totally radical compared to what others around you are doing with their lives.

Whatever it is, imagine if you'd just given it a go. Could your life have been totally different? Better maybe?

BE SHAMELESS

Well, read on and I'll show you how you can reach epic levels of awesomeness by just getting rid of the 'shame' gene and embracing the 'fuck it, let's do it' gene instead.

Remember, being shameless is not for everyone. But those who do embrace it are the ones who have the most stories to tell, and are some of the most successful.

Depending on where I am and what I am doing, I may or may not be doing something fun, boring, tiring, stupid or embarrassing.

Either way, I don't care anymore.

For a large majority of my life, what I did (or didn't do) was dictated by what people thought of me. Yet when I look back on all the instances when I made huge leaps in my life, achieved great things or did what anyone else would have classed as impossible, I had one overriding thought: fuck it!

I simply gave it a go.

I wasn't concerned if I looked like a complete plum, if it failed or embarrassed me; I just went for it. So far, I'm definitely 'in the black' with what I have achieved because of not worrying about what others thought. In fact, I got so into this way of living, I had a phrase tattooed on my leg: 'Death or Glory'. It's my own slightly morbid reminder that I'm all in or nothing.

I could use soooo many cheesy phrases right now, but annoyingly the one that sticks with me – and you'll know it – is that you miss 100% of the shots you don't take. It's so easy to create excuses why you don't 'do the thing', isn't it? I know, because that is exactly what I did for a long time.

It occurred to me some time ago, as I went through the transformation to where I am today, that quite frankly, pride will fuck you up!

Being too proud to ask for help, say you're struggling or have fucked up, ask the person you fancy out for dinner/drinks, go up to the speaker at the event, write the letter to your idol, make the connection that will change your life will simply Fuck. You. Up.

I really can't finesse it at all.

When I was too shy to say hello to *anyone* new for fear of what they may or may not have thought about me, I was essentially still 'happy'. But internally I was lonely as fuck and pretty depressed.

Years. It took me *years* to get over myself and actually realise that the worst thing that will happen is I will look like a bit of a knob. I have contacted people who are infinitely more successful, influential and – for all you youngsters reading this – more 'badass' than me. And do you know what the worst thing that someone has said to me is?

'I'm not interested.'

Followed by – well, nothing! (And I'll tell you what I do with those folks in another chapter, ha!)

But, and it's a big but, I have, by being shameless, managed to secure million pound contracts, written copy for some of the top names in fitness and marketing, funded my own fitness business, been invited to share a stage with big names speaking to hundreds (now thousands), and have clients all over the world.

Really – like proper really – when there's something you want to achieve in your life or business, what truly *is* the worst that can happen? I'll tell you one thing – your imagination can create some epically horrific shit, when in reality, it is never that bad.

So do me a favour. If there is something you have been putting off – a business you have had in your head; someone you want to connect with (on a business or romantic level) – just fucking do it! I can't stress enough how bad it *isn't* when you give it a try. I know, because I was a slave to the 'what if' gene which stopped me so many times going for things that – if I'd known then what I know now – I would have gone balls deep for!

Little 'what if' bastard. Don't let it stop you from creating the life that you deserve.

Oh, and you think asking for help, for connections, for guidance, admitting you have failed/fucked up and need a hand makes you weak or somehow a failure? Does it fuck! It makes you bloody smart, that's what it does.

Like I said, pride will fuck you up. I mean that 100%. Your ego, the annoying little shit, will prevent you from lowering your barriers and doing the one thing that will actually make a difference.

Shall I tell you what I have found? When you ask for help or admit things have gone wrong, people often help you – and help you willingly.

Why?

Put it this way – when you help someone, how do you feel? Crappy? Resentful? Like they owe you somehow? No, of course you don't (unless you are a *massive* tool). So when you ask for help/advice/guidance/assistance, you are *making the other person feel good, because it feels good to help people.*

Here is another great way of looking at it: if you don't let people help you and admit when you need a hand, you are actually a selfish arsehole because you are denying someone those good feelings.

I tell you what – when you've been knee deep in stripper shit, nothing seems too bad when it comes to being shameless.

I won't go into the story too much, but in my mid-twenties I fell out with my then boss and moved to London from Leeds. I found myself in London with the grand sum of £22 to live off. Now if you're not aware of London prices, to say 'fucking daft' would be an understatement.

So, I needed to make money, and pretty sharpish.

I'd put myself through university by having multiple jobs – from personal trainer to security guard to being a barman at a strip club. And before you say, 'Oh yeah, tits and booze, what could be better?' let me tell you one thing. What you see of strip clubs is glamorous – the reality ain't. I got the job because I ended up training a fair few of the ladies, and when they said I 'wasn't a creep' I got the gig.

A new club opened up just round the corner from me in London and, as I couldn't go back into the corporate world, I had to take what I could. So I walked in, suited and booted, and asked for work. Ended up being a floor manager.

So, imagine a club with 100+ women in it every night, plus customers, and it was a 'premium' environment so everything had to look and, well, *smell* the part. You know, there's a reason why they say not to flush sanitary products down the toilet – so that the damn toilet doesn't get blocked, and some poor floor manager (aka me) doesn't have to walk into the overriding smell of shit.

But I needed the job, I was broke, so I ended up creating a 'biohazard' suit out of bin bags, a woodworking mask and sunglasses.

And a stick.

Into the tank I went!

Not the highlight of my career, but you know what? I learned a valuable lesson because of 'Shitgate', as I like to call it. And that lesson is currently framed and standing up to the left hand side of the computer I am typing on.

It's a £10 note.

Why?

Well it was given to me by one of the dancers as a thank you for the horrid job I'd had to do (meaning they, in turn, could now work). This was at a time when Mum and Dad sent me a £15 voucher for a budget frozen food store and I walked round with a fucking calculator making every penny count. This was at a time when I would get to the club just before it opened, after the sandwich shop next door shut so I could get the ones they were throwing away before they went into the bin. This was at a time when £10 meant more to me than anything on the earth because I couldn't afford to fucking eat.

I didn't spend it.

I put it in my wallet where it remained for several years. Considering how skint I was back then, that does seem kinda dumb, doesn't it? Well this was me truly at my lowest – no money, no woman, *all* cry – yet I saved it.

I vowed that was the last £10 charity I would ever take, and if I had to spend it, that would be it. I would give up on any form of dream I had of making it and return home with my tail between my legs. It now serves as a reminder of how low life had been and to never, ever take for granted where I am now. It's my daily lesson never to let my life get to such a low point again.

Life isn't always going to be easy – in fact, if you are trying to better yourself or business in any way, be prepared for a pile of grief coming your way. Be willing and able to do the things that no one else will.

The thankless jobs.

The 'grunt work'.

The shit.

In my case, what doing that thankless job, knee deep in shit, gave me was hope – that and the massive kick in the pills I *really* needed to crack on and make some big changes in my life.

And I have applied this to every area of my life. I'll explain the story of how I got to work for him later on, but I ended up getting a gig under one of the biggest names in online marketing (and the smartest bastard I know too – bloody neuroscientist!). He didn't need me, but he had some thankless jobs that needed doing.

Now bear in mind at this time I still had a full-time personal training commitment in my gym and was training myself aggressively as a direct-response copywriter. I ended up doing several thousand customer care calls (the thankless task), from when I got home at 8pm until around 3/4am, Monday to Friday, then getting up at 6.30am to get back to the gym.

There was no money in it for me, but I was shameless, and seeing an opportunity where I could handle some work that nobody wanted to do, I pitched myself in. I did the work, and continued to do everything that was asked of me, from flying around the world to be at events and delivering 1,000+ 'turbo coaching' calls to writing 15,000 word sales letters in twenty-four hours at the weekend. All for free.

Daft, eh?

Well, as a result of my lack of shame, I ended up being coached by some of the world's best marketers/business people, learning skills that would have taken me easily five+ years to master, blowing up my network, and eventually landing a high five-figure a month contract to launch an agency on his behalf.

See, being shameless does pay off, eh? But more importantly, *I did the work*. The grunt work, to be exact. I put in the hours, with almost no expectation of anything in return. That and my lack of shame (or simply drinking enough at the time to ignore what I was about to do – I don't recommend this!) is the biggest contributor to where I am now.

And you wouldn't be reading this book if it wasn't for the sheer shamelessness and determination on my part.

Fact!

BE SHAMELESS TO DO/ACTION STEPS

Become shameless. This isn't for everyone, but those of you who do embrace it are the ones who will have the most stories to tell and be the most successful. Yes, you need to take pride in what you do, *but,* pride can fuck you up. Be humble in what you do otherwise it will come round and bite you in the arse (trust me).

Get the fuck over yourself. This is rather simple, but if you ask yourself in most scenarios nowadays, 'What's the worst that could happen?', likely it will be you look like a bit of a knob or someone saying, 'I'm not interested'. Your imagination can create some epically horrific shit, when in reality it's never that bad. You need to get over yourself and get out of your own way.

Do me a favour: if there's something you've been putting off for a while, just fucking do it!

Ask for help. Make other people feel good by asking for help. When you go out of your way and offer help, what happens? You feel *good*. Don't deny other people those same feelings. You'll find out quickly, when you ask for help or admit things have gone wrong, people will help you, and help you willingly. If you're struggling and feel like the weight of the world is all on your shoulders, go and ask for help from someone who knows how to get you over the hump.

3

BE WEIRD

(BUT NOT TOO FUCKING WEIRD)

The weird set an example for the rest of us. They
raise the bar. They show us through their actions
that in fact we're wired to do the new, not to comply
with someone a thousand miles away.
SETH GODIN

I want to share with you a concept of 'uniqueness'. Not
enough people understand it fully so I decided to dedicate a
whole chapter to it.

But first, let me run a couple of things by you, because you
may well be thinking shit, Dan, now I gotz ta be a weirdo too?
What you playing at? All I want to do is make wonga and play
video games all day.

Listen up.

Why do antiques and collectibles demand enough dinero to make a normal person weep? Or why are rare paintings swiped up for more than what an average person earns in a lifetime? Maybe that dress (yes, ladies, I know this publication until now has been very masculine. Sorry) which you pay over the odds for *just* because it's exclusive and one of a kind – why do these things happen?

Well because they are unique, one of a kind, limited edition, *singularis*.

And so for you, my friend, embracing your unique self, warts and all, is the single most beneficial thing you can do if you want to kick balls in life. When you are yourself, you are more than valuable – you are irreplaceable. There's no one else like you.

Fact.

I'm going to come straight out of the gate with this – I am *not* suggesting you act like an out-and-out oddball. We all knew the person at school who was quirky, a little different – they were cool. Then there was the one – you know, the weirdo who was just too strange. I'm all for dancing to your own beat – what I'm trying to say is if you think you're a bit odd, a bit different, a bit weird, that's great. Embrace it.

I know for a fact I am!

Look, when I started out in business – first in headhunting, then personal training, then copywriting and now the coaching/business/speaking/writing madness that is my life – I played it pretty straight. I've always been told I'm funny and that people seem to get on with me easily, but for far too long I tried to be someone I wasn't.

In fact, it got to the point where I had lived the lie for so long, I didn't know who I was anymore. I wanted to be this successful, sporty, badass tough guy who didn't give a shit and was all about 'living it large' and making money, but in real life, I'm quite geeky. I love being on my own and reading. Wandering around an aquarium listening to classical music is my idea of heaven. Spending all the monies buying miniatures in model stores and painting them is fucking awesome. Also pizza.

Don't get me wrong, I still like to tear the arse off a crazy night in Vegas, LA, or London, dancing absolutely terribly until the small hours and demolishing a mini bar and singing out loud in my boxers. But I would be just as happy figuring out if I can make bread.

See – hardly 'cool', is it?

But that's the thing. As entrepreneurs, I've found that we are all a bit odd. Which is great. I mean, let's face it – society, as a rule, expects us to go to school, go to college/university, get a job, work our way up, get a mortgage, a car, maybe get married and have kids – and keep this up till our late sixties when we can finally retire and do all the things we wanted to do. But then we get there and we're too tired, our knees don't work so well anymore, and it's all so…noisy.

And who knows? We might not even get to the wispy hair and cranky voice stage. 'Cause quite frankly, if there's one thing we *can't* control is our own mortality. So I say, surprise surprise, 'Fuck. That.'

We basically have (as an entrepreneur or someone who wants change) said to that scenario, 'Thanks, but no thanks. Not for me. I'll do my own thing. Now.' Turning your back on what is essentially the norm is a pretty fucking weird thing to do. Hence we are all a bit odd, eh?

Now I mentioned earlier that I tried to be something I am not for quite a while, and as much as I had seen people espousing the benefits of being myself, I thought, who on earth would be interested in me? I'm a bit of a dork.

Yeah, that's the kinda crap that holds so many back from achieving everything they want from life. It took time, don't get me wrong, but I started to be more me when I put my content out there. I wasn't afraid to share the highs and lows. I became Dan on the outside more and more, and as a result I became closer to the me that I was on the inside.

You know what the funny thing was? The more I was me, the more my audience grew and grew. The more I was me, the more people I connected with and could actually help. The more I was me, the more money flowed into my bank account. The more I was me, the more people identified with me and wanted to be a part of the journey.

My journey.

Crazy, eh?

All I had to do was stop hiding behind the mask I thought people wanted me to wear, stop giving quite so much of a fuck, and just be me. Warts and all. Good shit and bad shit.

The more honest I was with those I worked with, and my audience, the better life got, to the point where I use a cartoon of my ridiculous face on everything I create now (including, as you will have seen, this book). I'm going to ask that, over time, you stop trying to be who you think people want you to be.

The you inside – the one who has all the quirks and oddities and fuck-ups – be that person.

Be you!

You, when you're being you, are fucking awesome.

You, when you're trying to be someone or something else, are not awesome.

I'm not going to go all 'woo-woo' here, but figuring out who you are – why you are here, what your purpose is – is an absolute bitch. If you know all of that, fucking awesome! I know that for me, it's a work in progress.

As I have got older, what I stand for, what I believe in and who I essentially am has changed. And that's fine; people will see your progression and follow you regardless. We humans can smell bullshit and fakery from a mile away. But being genuinely you – well, that's a whole new ball game.

There's no one like you. You are unique. Your quirks are unique and your personality is unique. You're irreplaceable when you are genuinely you. And that's an awesome place to be as an entrepreneur/coach.

I can't stress this strongly enough: if you don't know who the real you is yet, start being the person who, deep inside, you have always wanted to be. Your uniqueness is what will draw people to you. Everyone loves a flawed hero.

I don't want perfect people. I want people who have a story, have been through some shit, dance to their own beat and still make it work, not the fake-arsed posh fuck-wits who look down on us slightly geeky weird-but-cool entrepreneurs.

BE WEIRD

A friend of mine gave me a great little sound bite, and he has turned this into a multi-million dollar business:

'Your mess is your message'.

All that stuff which you think is weird, embarrassing, or a failure – that's the exact stuff that people will bond with you over.

Why?

Because it makes *them* feel less weird. There are other weirdos *just* like them who have the balls/ovaries to put themselves out there.

We're human at the end of the day, and that's how we bond. Sooner or later the shit hits the fan for almost all of us, and it's these experiences that we can all resonate with.

I'll give you an example from my own life. When I had my first speaking gig I really wanted my personality to shine through, own the stage and make it a great experience for those watching. Instead, what I did was stand behind the lectern and deliver a PowerPoint presentation.

Yes, the content was good and I got great feedback, but looking back that must have been dull as piss – and I was hardly being myself.

Roll forward nearly three years. In front of a room of some extremely successful marketers and business owners, I proceeded to deliver a forty-five minute presentation wearing a Mexican wrestling mask and drinking vodka out of a crystal skull.

To be fair, I wasn't doing it for attention – I didn't know I was going to be on camera (let alone in front of so many people). It was 7pm and I looked a fucking state, and the only clean receptacle I had was a crystal skull acquired the night before. Old Dan would have been paranoid: 'What if people don't like me?'; 'What if people say bad things about me?'; 'What if they don't think I'm professional?'

Can you guess what happened?

I was widely regarded as one of the best, most entertaining and memorable speakers of the weekend. Floods of friend requests, new members on my site and a stack more presence followed.

Not bad for embracing my weird side, eh?

Look, you probably know if you are more on the introvert or extrovert scale (or the newly talked about 'entrepreneurial' personality that is gaining some serious ground). But you can find out about yourself in more scientific ways if you want.

I have put myself through the Kolbe, Myers-Briggs and DISC assessments, and these have been really useful in finding out who I am, what I'm good at and what makes me tick. Equally they've helped me grow and scale my businesses, as in the past I would have recruited people like me and invariably things would go tits up at some point. Now, as I know what I'm like in a more easy to understand way, I can recruit people who have the skills that I *don't* have, and as a result we have been able to scale fast.

When you know what your strengths and weaknesses are, you can leverage them, weirdness and all! Want some simple advice? If you are quiet, great with structure, very organised, partner up with someone who is outgoing, social, gregarious and a natural people person. It works well.

I will talk further about how to get your message out there later on, but before I sign off this chapter, I'm going to suggest you ease into it. Learn how to write compelling copy, how to tell a story, and possibly how to convey your message via video/camera. Take your time; it feels like you are getting a rectal exam to start with – very uncomfortable – but as time goes on, you will find your confidence growing and your message reaching more and more people.

Cool, eh?

Oh, and don't be one of those 'woe is me/my life is so shit/give me sympathy' people. Nobody likes those people.

Use your sorrows and pain as your strength, because that's exactly what they are. You've come out a better human. Embrace the new you and share with the world your weird but wonderful tales of bravery and triumph. (OK, sorry to go slightly *Game Of Thrones* style there.)

BE WEIRD TO DO/ACTION STEPS

Figure out what your strengths and weaknesses are. Play to your strengths and find people who can help you with your weaknesses. By doing this you can leverage your time and what you're amazing at. Don't be the person who tries to do everything and spreads themselves so thinly they become part of the noise.

Start living the genuine you. Don't try and fake who you are. Spend time figuring out and getting to know who the real you is. Start being that person – the person inside of you. The person you've always wanted to be. Your uniqueness is what will draw people to love you (or hate you).

Stop right now trying to be the person you think people want you to be. Take the time to figure out who you are, why you are here and what your purpose is. And yes, it's an absolute bitch.

4

BE BRUTALLY HONEST

As I have said, the first thing is to be honest with
yourself. You can never have an impact on society if
you have not changed yourself first...
NELSON MANDELA

This perhaps is one of the easiest chapters to write, but I guarantee you that this is one of the hardest things to actually *do*.

Unfortunately, many of us say that we are honest with ourselves, but really? As in proper really?

Most people are full of shit.

We aren't honest with ourselves. And hence, when we have our legs hanging in the grave, we realise, 'Shit, I lied to myself my whole life.'

What a waste.

I'm also going to show you why the 'follow your passion' advice can sometimes be a load of bollocks. Not that many people have a true passion that can be monetised (some rare cases, but very few). They may be interested in something, or like doing something, but passion? Well, that's too much of a strong word.

And that's exactly why it backfires. People use it as a crutch and excuse as to why they haven't done anything with their life.

'Oh, I haven't found anything that I'm passionate about so I'm still looking.'

Fuck that! There's no such thing.

Work with your interests and things you like, observe whether the market wants what you have and put it out there. The passion will come later. You'll start loving what you do once you're good at it and it makes you feel good to be contributing to people.

Now, I'm essentially going to beat you down with two exercises, and if you have the balls/ovaries to do them, you will probably hate me for a bit. The first exercise is going to help you understand your situation right now; the second is going to put it all in perspective.

I've said it before: if you are 100% happy with your lot in life, I really am happy for you. But I'm guessing, as you're reading this book, that you're probably thinking there could be something more to life.

I will bring you back up, but this next bit might hurt a little. In fact, this chapter is a down right beat down. Soz.

But it's really very simple.

The now. Take a look at your bank balance, savings, investments and assets. That is a direct reflection of how successful you are financially.

Take a look in the mirror, in your smalls. That is a direct reflection – literally – of how well you take care of yourself (obviously medical conditions excluded).

Take a look around you when you go to bed at night. Is there anyone next to you? Do you have kids in the house? That is a direct reflection of the investment in your personal/intimate relationships.

Please note: not everyone wants a partner, to have a family and so on – but if you do, I am just highlighting the fact.

Take a look in your inbox, text messages and social calendar. That is a direct reflection of the time you have invested in your friendships.

How did that feel?

I'm sure some of you reading this will think, ha, you bearded twat, I'm awesome in all those areas. If you are, good for you! I know I'm not, but I also know the areas that I am weak on now.

There has been more than one occasion when I have got to the end of the day of work with a newly acquired gut hanging over the sides of my jeans, gone to bed totally alone, having no one to ask me out for a pint or simply to hang out, with maxed credits cards and just the cash in my 'oh fuck, you really have messed up now, Dan' stash at home. So yeah, I have been there. I'm still there in some ways...

But every day I look at the above list (I really do) and try to move the needle towards what I see as my ideal life. Is it quick? Is it balls! There is only so much time in the day, but not knowing (and we'll come to that in a bit) is a bugger. Painful as it is, it's better to have a completely clear – albeit possibly shitty – picture of where you are right now.

I mean, how can you expect to achieve anything if you have no idea where you are starting? Trust me, I kidded myself for far too long. It is painful, but I know for a fact it's the best thing you can do. Not knowing where you stand and where you are coming from is a sure fire way to wither away into oblivion. And that's not what I want for you. Heck, that's not what *you* want, I'm guessing.

You wanna be awesome, build a great business and have the freedom to do all the things your heart desires. But it starts with being brutally honest with yourself. We can lie to the world, but never to ourselves. So don't be a douche and skip this; give it time, and slowly make a plan to change those areas of your life that you're not happy with.

If you want a truly brutal version of this exercise, go online and download one of those form builders. Make it so the replies are anonymous and send the link to your partner (a bold move!), friends, exes (argh!), colleagues and associates. Ask them to tell you a) what they really think of you, and b) how you could improve.

Ouch!

I did this once, and if my balls were digitised, they would be flat as a pancake from the kicks. It was brutal! But, it gave me the feedback I needed to make the changes to be a better version of myself.

It comes down to the concept of 'unconscious incompetence'. If you don't know what you don't know, how can you improve?

Food for thought.

The future (and putting it all in perspective). (I believe I learned this from a Dan Kennedy piece, but I can't be sure as it's been with me a fair while.)

You will need some squared paper for this – or you can print out some boxes on a spreadsheet. You then need to partition off a number of boxes.

As I am a Brit, the number that I will be using is eighty-two.

What is that?

Well, it's the average life expectancy of a person living in the UK right now.

Next thing you want to do is colour in as many squares as you are old.

Done?

OK, what isn't coloured is a rough estimation of how long you have left on this planet (assuming you survive all the other stuff life throws your way in the meantime).

How many have you got? As of writing this I have forty-seven squares left to play with.

Let's knock off, say, seventeen, which takes me to sixty-five (if I was to retire, as it were). And at that age, I imagine I won't have the energy and drive I do now. So with that in hand, I currently have thirty squares.

Thirty squares to make a difference.

Seems like quite a lot, right?

Well, I can remember going to watch *Short Circuit* when I was eight, then my birthday party at eighteen, dancing quite drunkenly to 'Tequila' by Terrorvision at twenty-one, moving to London when I was twenty-seven, moving back home when I was thirty-one as a personal trainer, opening my gym at thirty-three and being on stage in NYC at thirty-five.

Those are all the things that I can remember. (Lol – I had a *lot* of head trauma when I played rugby, ha! That and, you know, vodka.)

I'm being a plum, of course, but shit! I genuinely remember being a teenager, and now I'm on the wrong side of my thirties writing this.

Time. Goes. Faster. Than. You. Think.

And I swear it speeds up as you get older. One thing I have learned from speaking to old folks (and you really should spend time with people in the seventy+ bracket; the advice you can get from them is gold), is that those who worked really hard usually wish they'd spent more time with their loved ones and not worked quite so much. Which is why in the previous chapter I stressed how important it is to schedule that in.

However, regret for the things they didn't do was equally massive.

Don't go to your grave with regrets!

It's already a dark fucking place. You don't wanna add more doom and gloom to the mix, you know. I'm serious. You are only here – relatively speaking – for a very short time. In the grand scheme of things, we are gone in a blink when you compare our life to how long the universe has been here.

Now, this may all seem a bit morbid. For a long time I had a real crippling fear of death. I have found – with those who are open enough to share it – it's quite common. If you are religious, that's awesome; you know what you have in store. But for the rest of us? It's a great big bastard unknown and that can be truly terrifying.

Until you accept it, that is.

When you realise no matter what you do, it's going to happen eventually, it's liberating. You may be able to make your life last longer by keeping yourself fit and healthy, but one day – that's it. Time's up.

When I finally thought, fuck it, and accepted that I have just one roll of the dice, I realised I had better make it count. And finally I started to experience the success I had always wanted.

My philosophy? We started off as a bunch of atoms. We are, one day, going to end up as a bunch of atoms. So why worry?

Really, worrying about what people think, if you fuck up, if you look stupid, if it doesn't work, if they say no, in the grand scheme of things is pointless. Honestly, you have so little to lose. Let go of all the bullshit stories you are telling yourself about why X or Y won't work and give it a fucking go! We're all gonna end up a decomposed mush underground anyway (or burned up in smoke for the fire loving peepz).

Look, not everyone can change the world, right? But can you make a difference to a handful of people, or 100, or maybe 1,000? Of course you can. If you better yourself, do good work, help people and take chances, one day you will get there.

That's the thing. I speak to people who want to help a million people, break a new country, change the face of whatever thing they are into. But what's wrong with starting small? Help yourself first, then try to help a few more people, and go from there.

In life you don't get a trophy for taking part (which I think is a pile of wank anyway). Humans evolved with rather awesome brains that made us pretty smart and good problem solvers. Why have so many people seemingly lost the art of discovery? Of wanting to know how things work? Of simply looking at stuff and thinking: I can do that better?

If you think you can make a difference, have a great idea or have something awesome that you want to get out there, then let me tell you something. This could be one of the most important things I could ever tell you, and something I wish I had twigged earlier:

'You need no-one's permission' (with the caveat that we ain't here that long). So why are you waiting for someone to tell you it's OK to do the thing?

Just fucking do it!

It is *your* life. It is yours to do with as you damn well see fit. You don't have to be a crazily driven nut bag like me, but if you are feeling unfulfilled, or that you either want or deserve more out of life, then go get it, bulldog!

As I have said before, I have been blessed to spend a lot of time around some very successful and smart people. People I look up to. Not that much different to you or me, except they're geniuses, as in proper ones. They are from another planet, I think.

They had an idea, a vision, a dream, a goal…and they just went for it.

Really, that's the difference I found between them and me when I was looking for the answer. That, and work.

A lot of hard work.

Again I come back to the fact that I am selling some very unsexy ideas with this book. The fact is that there's no easy way out, no short cut, no 'push button here for money' system. You are going to have to accept the fact that, if you want to change any part of your life, it is going to take hard work and a degree of sacrifice on your part.

Now, this next section is in direct contradiction to a lot of the wispy nonsense I read online:

Follow your passion. Yawn. Look, my passions are eating pizza, watching cartoons, sleeping and being naked with the opposite sex. Is anyone going to pay me for that?

Are they bollocks. (Besides, there is a *lot* of hair…)

You need to be real, especially if you are dipping your toe into the entrepreneurial world. In fact, does anyone even want to buy your shit? Just because you can make amazing cakes out of wasps (no idea where that came from) or have a 'revolutionary' new system for something, does anybody actually want what you are putting out there?

I am not trying to dissuade you from going for whatever it is that you want to do, but bear in mind it would be nice if people actually wanted to buy it, right?

There are lots of ways you can find out: hanging around on the forums of your target market, Facebook groups, web searches, surveys, in-person chats, Google hangouts – you name it. Sometimes you have an amazing idea and you can knock it out of the park, make all of the millions and live the dream. Sometimes you come up with something that is OK, makes you a living, and that's fine too. Sometimes you come up with an idea, and it's utter crap. But without testing, you'll never know.

Being brutally honest with yourself as you go through this process is key to not ruining yourself, your life or your reputation. I am all for giving it a go – I mean, I have built my career on that – but just because someone says, 'Follow your passion' doesn't mean it has fuck all to do with real life.

I shared this in my private membership group the other day and, considering how many comments I usually get on my posts, this one was 'meh' at best. It was the world's simplest business plan (and FYI I *hate* business plans, but that's for another time. Useless things as a rule!):

1. Find a group of people who are in pain (physical, financial, mental – basically people who have a need of some description).
2. Spend time interacting with them, find out exactly what that need is, and then research the crap out of it.
3. Go away, create a product, system or solution that serves the need.
4. Sell it to them.

Hardly rocket science, hardly tricky, not sexy, and I can't turn that into a course worth thousands, can I? But if you want a profitable business that has an impact, makes a difference and serves people – see those four points?

Go do that.

End of.

BE BRUTALLY HONEST TO DO/ACTION STEPS

Figure out where you're at right now. Take a look at aspects of your life (bank balance, the mirror and how you take care of yourself, relationships and friendships) and do an audit on yourself. You need to figure out where you're at *right now*. Be brutally honest with yourself.

Make a plan to change those areas you aren't happy with. Again you need to be brutally honest with yourself, and you're going to have to give this time. For the truly brutal version, download an online form builder. Set replies to anonymous and send the link to friends, partner and work colleagues. Ask them to tell you what they really think of you and how you could improve.

A fast way to see how long you have left on this planet (and it's nowhere near as long as you think). Grab some squared paper, or print similar off. Partition off a number of boxes. Use eighty-two as an example (average Brit life expectancy). Next, colour in as many boxes as your age. What isn't coloured is how long you have left. Time goes faster than you think.

You need no one's permission. Whatever it is, if you're waiting for someone to tell you it's OK for you to do something, fuck it and go and do it. Accept you have one roll of the dice called Life and I guarantee you'll start to experience success in ways you never would have expected. Do not give a fuck about what others will think.

THE WORLD'S MOST SIMPLE BUSINESS MODEL (DO THIS):

- Find people who are in pain: people who have a need.
- Interact with them and find out exactly what the need is.
- Go and research it.
- Create a product that serves the specific need.
- Sell it to them.

5

BE VALUABLE

Investing in yourself is the best investment you will
ever make. It will not only improve your life, it will
improve the lives of all those around you.
ROBIN S. SHARMA

Why do people baulk at the suggestion of investing in
themselves and their skills, but are perfectly ready to smack
down £10k+ on cars and material things?

It's funny how we stop learning and making ourselves more
and more valuable as soon as we hear that last bell ringing in
the school hallways. But then we expect to have the same
luxury life as the big, successful people of the world who, to
be frank, are *always* investing in themselves to improve a skill,
learn something new, or even get one nugget of info which
will keep them progressing in their game.

In this chapter I want to share some of my insights on how you need to master your skills and identify your weaknesses to scale up your business pursuits.

No country was conquered by one person, it takes armies. So become the general and strategically recruit people to your mission. It's the best and only way you'll be able to scale up and become totally awesome.

Did you go to school? I am assuming you have experienced formal education to some degree. Whether you left in your teens, twenties or later, how much time, money and effort have you invested in your skills since you left the formal structure?

Put it this way. I did my A-levels in Double Maths, Physics and Design. I wanted to be an engineer. As you can see, I didn't end up being one.

Then I wanted to be a personal trainer, so I spent my student loan on the relevant qualifications. Although I wasn't the prettiest of the bunch (I didn't walk around with a six-pack, tanned orange and squeezed into Lycra so tight that quite frankly you could see all my junk), I was a big, strong bearded lump, and I did pretty damn well.

After I'd opened my facility, next on the agenda was copywriting. Now I certainly wasn't trained in this world, but I found those who were, went to seminars, watched online trainings, bought courses and went in balls deep, putting in five–seven hours a day on top of my day job to get as good as I could, as fast as I could.

This has continued as I have grown my businesses. In fact, I invest all my time and a small bastard fortune on my skills to make sure that I serve my clients to the highest possible levels. That and develop as a businessman and person as a whole.

Which brings me to my next point, and something that I find rather silly: if you are a twenty-year-old life coach, you can, quite frankly, fuck off!

If I want someone to life coach me in this instance, I would want them to have – well – had a life.

This reminds me of someone I heard about a while back who was marketing themselves as an 'Ultimate Man Coach' (whatever that is). *Really?*

If I was to invest in someone with their shit together, I would want them looking good, with multiple successful businesses, life on their own terms, a great social life, hot-as-balls wife, cool kids and generally living the dream. Except this prize plum was earning barely a grand a month, had no missus and still lived with his mum.

Lol!

See what I mean?

A lot of people want to launch a business, go online, pitch some amazing product and make all the monies. I'm all for that, and history of society is littered with many examples of relatively young people who have absolutely killed it. But what is wrong with finding something you are good at, have a talent for, and then getting *really fucking good at it*?

We all want instant success, fast results, quick fixes – we are human, after all. But you know what? The people who end up being really successful in the long run spend a lot of time honing their craft, learning, adapting (just because something worked yesterday doesn't mean it's going to work tomorrow), investing in themselves and failing over and over again. With time, these people become bloody good at what they do and can then charge premium fees.

I see a *lot* of advertising about people offering training courses for selling high-ticket, big-package items (I have one too, but I'll come to that in a mo.), but have they really got the skills or talents to warrant charging monstrous fees? Or are they just screwing folks over?

Now they might be a prodigy who has some crazy skills for whatever it is they are selling. But, most of us aren't fucking Mozart. Most of us maybe have a knack for something, or may like something enough to get really good at doing it, but it takes time to get *really* good – like mastery-level good.

With my courses, I teach people to get paid what they are worth and position themselves as the premier option in their niche, but not at the expense of quality or service. We all start somewhere. When I was a PT I started off charging £15/hour; when I last did it, I was around the £100 mark. Same with my coaching. It started off roughly around a few hundred a call. Now I can command four-figures for half the time because I actually have the skills to deliver a result worth that sum.

I could *not* have done this at twenty, fo sho.

There have been multiple books and studies done on the subject of mastery and the '10,000 hour rule'. And I am all for that. I did several thousand (I think it was around 13,000 in the end) hours of personal training, hence I felt I was pretty damn good and justified the prices I charged at the time.

When I went into copywriting, I didn't have that long. In fact, I first started charging after almost five months. I came out the gate with a pretty robust price too. Why? Well, I had been writing sales emails and adverts for years with my recruitment and advertising jobs, and I literally lived and breathed the copywriting world for the months I was training.

Really, I was a proper weirdo about it.

I was honest with my clients. I was confident in my abilities but I never positioned myself as the best. Just really good.

And, if it didn't work or convert as planned, I would work my nuts off until it did.

Again, honesty for the win!

Which brings us to a topic that is often bandied around: the concept of 'faking it till you make it'.

In part, I agree with this. You need to adopt the mindset, behaviour and attitude of those who are successful until they become ingrained. But, as much as you can roll a turd in glitter and put it in a box with a bow around it, it is still a turd. You *have* to have skill or talent for something before you can charge people for it, otherwise you are just a con artist peddling snake oil.

You can *definitely* position yourself in a way so as not to come across as desperate for business – and you can do that with a variety of application processes, not being needy and at the beck and call of your customers or prospects. But you *have* to invest in your skills and continually develop them if you want to make it.

Dan's rule of making it. Two years *minimum*. Two years of continual hard work, education, trial and error, networking, a degree of sacrifice, focus, discipline and drive towards your end goal.

I worked for *free* for Ryan Levesque for nearly a year on top of my day job, delivering coaching and personal development. I did this because he was a true master, was several years ahead of me in his craft, and I had a chance to learn at his feet. As a result, this sped up the time it took me to be pretty good at stuff.

I was anything but polished (I am still not, ha), but he saw a raw skill in me and pushed me – literally – to my limits to help me level up my skills. I did the jobs no one else wanted to do, as I've said before, but I got a first class education in copy, marketing, funnels, business and team building in the process.

I don't know if I could put a price on it, because if it weren't for that, I wouldn't be here now. It was, in fact, my tipping point.

Don't get me wrong – my two-year rule can be bent. If you look back at my journey, when I decided to go online, the first thing I wanted was to be a badass copywriter. Then I wanted to be an expert funnel builder. Then I got kinda good at coaching in this space. In turn, I developed that skill to the point I am at now, where I am not too shabby at it.

Am I the finished product?

No.

Far from it. At best I'm half way; I still have a lot to learn about growing businesses (so I can one day sell 'em), management, finessing my copy and coaching. Hence, I spend thousands each month on courses and coaching for myself and my team to try to get as good as I/we can.

Which leads me on to my next point:

Be a producer, and not just a consumer. There I go with the contradictions again. Of course you have to invest in your education and skills, I'm not saying don't do that. But there has to be a point where you go from consuming the information to actually putting what you know into practice by producing something of value.

Which is where most people fuck up.

They buy course after course, and they have a product, their own course or system – whatever – that they want to get out there in the world. And guess what?

It stays on their desktop.

No one sees it.

No one buys it.

No one benefits from it.

Pretty sad, really, to have invested all that time and effort into creating something and not getting it out there in the world. Criminal, but that's the reality.

So, I'm going to introduce you to two concepts I have lived by, and a little dirty insider tip which will probably surprise you, but you should embrace it if you wanna get ahead.

The first concept is: speed to market beats perfection.

The second one is: it's OK to be shit at stuff.

Let's start with the first one. There is a reason I have achieved a degree of success pretty quickly. I didn't know I did this, but after reading the book *Ready, Fire, Aim* by Michael Masterson, I realised this was exactly what I had done.

Essentially what I do is have an idea, do my research, see if there is a market for it, if I can deliver it and if it will be good. Then I go ahead and launch the fucker.

I am a huge fan of crazy arbitrary deadlines, leveraging social proof (and the fear of looking like an absolute tit if I don't do it) and pushing limits, boundaries and expectations. Mainly because I enjoy it. But secondly, because I know it trumps perfection and consuming content. Every. Single. Time.

Most people spend so long trying to make their thing perfect, they never get it out there. Me? I aim to get whatever it is 60–

80% perfect, and as long as the customer is happy and they get the desired result, I'm happy. Then, as time goes by, I refine, tweak, adjust and, if needed, completely redo whatever needs attention. Hence the order of the words 'ready, fire, aim'.

Whatever you want to create, launch or show the world, if you have it, get it out there now. If you don't have it, get ready and tell the world you are going to get it out there by X date. And then fucking do it!

Seriously, I have had hundreds of coaching calls where this is exactly the problem. So what if it's not perfect? So what if it's not exactly how you envisioned it? If it helps people, solves a problem or makes a difference, *get it the fuck out there.*

I hope I have made my point clear.

So earlier on I promised you a dirty little secret.

Now, bear in mind I have hung out with authors, product creators, and online course experts – you name it. And not everyone does this, but you know what?

Some people sell you something that doesn't even exist yet!

That's right: you are buying something that isn't actually there.

BE VALUABLE

This is brilliant for you to understand.

Let's say you have the skills and talents to teach/create something, and you have an audience you know would like it. Wouldn't it be easier to find out if people want what you are selling before going to all the trouble of making it? Damn right, it would!

So, you put it out there. If no one buys, or just a handful of folks buy, no drama. You refund them. But if enough people invest, to the point where you think, fuck, this could be a thing, then you know full well that you *have* to get it done now. Or, you will look like a dick.

And you don't want to look like a dick, do you?

Course not.

If you go this route, write some sales copy, get it out in the world (social media, your local community, paid advertising, etc.), tell everyone when it will be ready – that's your thing – and make sure you work your balls/ovaries off to deliver it. Like I said, if not enough people buy, just be honest. There wasn't enough interest to run it this time, so here's your money back. No harm done.

Or, if you are smart, and you have a few folks who really want it, you could ask them to try and recruit a few more folks to make it viable.

Just a thought.

I want to make something very clear – you will *never* be perfect. You will *never* be good at everything. There are some things that you will simply suck at.

And it's OK. To be shit is A-O-K.

I did OK across the industries I worked in, but it wasn't until I dropped the ego and realised I was utterly dire at certain things that I was finally able to experience the crazy business growth I have now.

I am really good with people.

I am really good at sales.

I am really good with words.

I am really good at building tribes and getting people together.

I am crap at systems.

I am crap at organising myself.

I am crap at long term (past 3-6 months) planning.

I am crap at singing.

As I have said before, it makes sense to work on your weaknesses, but only to a degree. Me, personally? I prefer to know my strengths, get really good at them and then find someone else to handle my weaknesses.

And if you really analyse some of the big shots out there in the world, that's exactly what they do too. You can't build empires if you keep doing everything yourself.

The reason to work on your weaknesses a bit is so that, when you recruit or outsource stuff, you know what's good and what's bad. So for me, to start with I got a PA to organise my life day to day, an operations manager to take my crazy ideas, make them reality, and kick my arse so I didn't miss anything, and a personal trainer/cook to make sure I didn't turn into a fat mess again.

It may sound easy for me to say this now I have a few pennies, and it's very easy to say, 'Get stuffed, Dan, I don't have money for things like that!' Well, I didn't either when I started.

But I had skills, time, energy. So, I swapped them. I would either partner up with someone (in a business capacity) who complemented me by having the skills I was rubbish at and create a joint venture, or I would offer my skills (at points sales, marketing, copywriting and personal training) in return for their expertise.

It's only your shame that will stop you doing this. Like anything in life, you have no idea what you can get unless you ask.

I know it seems like a lot, but it boils down to finding something you are good at, getting really good at it, using that skill to get something to market, then finding folks who complement your lack of skills (pay 'em or swap stuff for 'em). And there you go.

Job done!

BE VALUABLE TO DO/ACTION STEPS

Fake it till you make it – a bit. You're going to need to adopt the mindset, behaviour and attitude of those you look up to and who are successful until it becomes ingrained.

You have to have a skill/talent. Find out what you're really fucking good at. Invest your time and energy sharpening your skills *before* you charge people for them. If you want to make it, you're going to need to be continually investing to develop your skills.

But there comes a point where you need to stop consuming and start producing something of value to your audience. Ask your audience if they actually want what you have before you create it to save time. Get something of value the fuck out there even if it's not perfect.

Work on your weaknesses (just a little bit). Figure out where your strengths and weaknesses are. Don't try and do everything yourself. Whatever you know you aren't that good at, outsource it and find someone who is the dog's bollocks so you can focus on your strengths. My bat shit talent happens to be coaching, so I outsource most other things.

6

BE INTERESTING

You can close more business in two months by
becoming interested in other people, than you can in
two years by trying to get people interested in you.
DALE CARNEGIE

Seems like a bit of an odd concept, doesn't it, 'be interesting'?
But bear with me, this is really bloody important.

In this chapter I want to share why to be interesting, you have
to be interested, and answer questions such as: 'Dan, how can
I come across as a well-rounded, interesting guy/gal who
people want to be around?' or 'I've been wanting to get X
client on board. How can I get him to cave in to my
product/service?'

I'll show you exactly how you can do that in a bit. But first,
take a look around. The people who have the most friends, a
huge network, or own successful businesses are in fact
extremely interesting. They know how to start and keep a

conversation; they are well-rounded individuals, and they can talk on various topics. But most of all, if they don't know something, they will become interested. They will ask you; they'll probe and really try their best to become interested in what lights your fire.

In such a crazy, fast-paced, hyper-connected world it is getting harder and harder to stand out. In fact, with thousands of contacts across all manner of platforms, it's really easy to forget about people. And be forgotten, full stop.

Which is why being a) interesting yourself, but more importantly b) interested in others is crucial.

I'll show you how to do that shortly.

As I mentioned earlier, people have lost the art, or even concept, of figuring shit out, seeing how things work or questioning the status quo. I see people who are quite content to talk about and use stuff when they have no bloody idea *what* they are talking about.

Makes me sad.

We are, by our very nature as humans, inquisitive buggers, and although I'm not saying you have to know how everything works, having a broad understanding of the world and what's in it will do wonders for you.

I used to be very closed minded to things. I had, in my mind, what I thought was right/wrong, good/bad, interesting/dull all figured out. And that is what we call a 'fixed mindset'.

Aka – a shit mindset.

Now? I have what's called a 'growth mindset'. In the real world that means I have my own ideas, values, interests and thoughts, but I am not averse to modifying or changing them.

I said earlier that I have truly embraced the fact that I am not cool, and if not being cool means I am who I am now – fuck, I'm all for it. I learn from a variety of sources; below is just an example of the things I consume, places I go, and stuff I do:

- Visit art galleries and museums
- Read history books and texts
- Devour autobiographies and biographies of people I admire who exhibit the character traits I value
- Take classes on anything that takes my fancy (I recently signed up for a stand-up comedy class. *What?*)
- Keep up to date on current affairs
- Study finance, the markets and business in general
- Hang out with old folks who have done stuff with their lives
- Go to watch opera, plays and dramas
- Study philosophy and some of the great thinkers of our time and past times

- Travel to fucking weird places where I can't speak the language and hang out with the locals
- Watch documentaries on some of the weirdest subjects you can imagine

This list probably comes as a surprise if you know me in real life or have interacted with me on social media.

I am by no means a culture vulture. Equally, throwing in some dumb, crazy, dangerous or plain weird shit is great too. I have a pretty decent online community, and they love it when I do daft things to share with them. Some of the highlights have been:

- Being mischievous at the Playboy mansion and posing in the grotto
- Hiring a limo and a lady driver for the day to take me sightseeing around LA
- Going to a 'challenge' food restaurant and filming the results
- Watching classical music in the natural history museum dressed as a dinosaur
- Holding a mastermind on a boat with everyone dressed as pirates and drinking rum
- Being cycled around San Diego by a tiny woman (with my meaty friend) at 2am singing 'Build Me Up, Buttercup'
- Waterboarding... myself.

You see, since I've dropped that cool mask and embraced everything this rather nuts planet has to offer, not only do I feel I am a more rounded individual, but I have a lot more to offer in conversations. I can come up with some really creative copy and stories, and people tell me I'm not just fun to be around, but actually interesting.

I have a lot of fun too. The odd bit of trouble, but nothing I can't get out of. Oh, and a fair bit of mischief, ha!

Weird that, eh?

In fact, when it comes to meeting people (and boy, do I have a beast of a method to connect with people and build rapport fast), one of my favourite things to do is judge them on sight. From what they wear, to what they write, to how they carry themselves, to what they believe in – judge, judge, judge!

Then, I take that judgment and totally put it to one side. Because I absolutely *love* being proven completely wrong.

There is nothing better than meeting someone who comes across as a quiet, shy and introverted person, but actually turns out to be a super successful business person, or a meathead strongman who is completing his PHD. Or an enhanced stripper who is a published author, artist and public speaker. (All three are, in fact, friends of mine – if you are reading, you know who you are, ha!)

So by going from a fixed mindset to a growth mindset, I have made more friends, more money, had more success, am happier and feel I am a better person. So, maybe give that a spin yourself.

Right, I promised you a few tips on how to connect with people and build rapport. Firstly, I am going to go back to a lesson my dad taught me when I was in the car with him during his sales calls:

'Son, you have two ears and one mouth for a reason'.

Like a lot of the advice I give, this may seem overly simple, but how many of you actually follow it? In fact, it is the easiest way to be seen as interesting by other people – take an interest in them!

Another great quote, which directly applies to this and how I build genuine rapport and connection so fast, is:

'If you want to be interesting, be interested'.

Now, you can't fake this. You have to – as I do – have a genuine interest in other people, their stories and what makes them tick. Most people in a conversation, whether that be verbal or written, are simply waiting for either the next chance to speak or to hammer home their point/thoughts/ideas.

Not. Ideal.

So, how do you (and I hate myself for using this word as it's soooo overused) 'hack' this communications conundrum?

Simple. Like *really* fucking simple.

Firstly, listen more than you speak. I can't make that any fancier. Let people talk more than you talk to them. I could explain why, but you don't need to know. You just need to do.

Secondly, if you are meeting someone for the first time – again, doesn't matter if it's in person or online – near the start of the conversation, a variation of the below I find works like stink:

'So, how do you spend your time?'

Huh? Is that it?

Yep.

OK, I have been using this for a long time. Normally the standard question when meeting someone for the first time is 'What do you do?' which means the only subject you have to kick things off is work.

However, with the question I showed you, depending on the response you can immediately tailor the conversation to what *the other person* is interested in. What really lights their fire? And as you know, people *love* talking about themselves. So why not be a smart arse and use this to your advantage?

Let me explain. If they start talking about work, you kick things off with work chats. Spending time with family? Ask them how they like being a parent, how old their kids are, how long they have been with a partner. They like tearing the arse out of a weekend and going on a three-day bender? Well, find out where they go, what they like to do and what's the most fun night they have had while arse-tearing, as it were.

Another great tip: let's say someone is really interested in model car making and racing. This actually happened to me in my headhunting days with a *very* senior director, but I had no idea about, or the slightest bit of interest in, this topic.

Remember earlier I said I enjoyed getting to know what makes people tick? This is a really good practice to adopt.

Instead of trying to fake it – and as he was a massive fan, he would have spotted my bullshit a mile off – I simply said, 'I used to have one of those when I was a kid. I had no idea people raced them. Tell me, how did you get into it? Where did you start?'

At the beginning of the call he had told me he had a meeting to go to in five minutes; he ended up speaking for almost an hour. I simply shut the fuck up, was genuinely interested in his passion, and let him talk.

From then on I was his favourite recruiter. In fact, the account was worth around half a million to the firm I worked for at the time, and a fair chunk of commission came to me. Goes to show, it's not all about you. And I am all for being an interesting, gregarious and entertaining person, but pipe down, ask questions about the other person, and actually listen. You will be amazed at the benefits to you.

In fact, the feeling of importance and being listened to is so profound that Dale Carnegie even mentions it in his book *How To Win Friends and Influence People*. (If you don't have it, buy it!).

People like to feel important, and you being genuinely interested in their shit gives them that feeling.

Books. Pretty much every successful person I meet nowadays is well read, and from – as you may have guessed – a variety of sources.

If you like audiobooks, good for you, but I tend to find I am doing other stuff when I'm listening to them. So I prefer actual books, made out of paper.

I have around 700ish at the moment, and I know a fair few of my friends have the same obsession, but I end up feeling guilty that I haven't read them.

In my opinion, if you get even one good idea or big takeaway from a book, it has served its purpose. You don't have to read it cover to cover. You can read the chapters that are relevant to you at this moment in time. Or even just the summaries. Sometimes the title of the book gives you all you need.

Now one thing I want you to get over is treating books like they are precious sweet little nothings. Don't be afraid to mark or highlight them. The knowledge is sure, but I was taught a system that works really well. And I'm going to give it to you.

Have a notepad (I have a big leather bastard which I call 'The Tome' where everything gets written), some Post-it notes, some sticky page tabs, a retractable pencil and a highlighter.

See a passage that's important? Highlight the fucker.

Had a great idea after reading something? Whack a Post-it note on it with your idea.

Need to make some notes on what you've read? Get that pencil out and write in the margins.

Stick a tab on each page where you have done something, then once you have finished, take your ideas, notes, scribbles and thoughts and write them up in your Tome. What you get is a fucking awesome highlights reel of everything you have learned. And if you are ever stuck for ideas, get your Tome out and get inspired.

Smart, eh?

Stories. The final part of this chapter is about the concept of storytelling. Whether it be a short anecdote or a long and winding tale, getting good at telling stories is something I would advise you to do.

Ever since we lived in caves we have passed on information through stories. It's hard-wired into our DNA to learn from stories. If you are not a natural storyteller, don't worry – it's not a problem. There are lots of books and resources to help you spin a better yarn.

Something I'm doing is getting trained in stand-up comedy and comedy writing. Why? Well, making people laugh is one of the hardest things you can do. So, if you can make people laugh with what you say and write, you're on to a winner.

So in closing, to learn how to be interesting, be interested in others. End of.

BE INTERESTING TO DO/ACTION STEPS

If you're meeting someone for the first time. Near the start of the conversation, ask them, 'How do you spend your time?' Simple. People love to talk about themselves. Asking this question will lead them to talk about what they love.

My system for taking relevant and useable notes from books. I don't want you to be afraid of marking your books. Have a notepad at the ready, some Post-it notes, sticky page tabs, pencil and highlighter. If you see something that's important, highlight the fucker and whack a Post-it note on with your idea. Take your ideas and add them to your master notebook – your 'Tome'.

Learn the art of storytelling. You need to get good at telling stories and it's something I advise you do. If you can make people laugh with what you say and write, you're on to a winner. And everyone has a story, so don't tell me you don't. Your life is your story.

7

BE SPITEFUL

(PROVE 'EM WRONG)

Don't worry about the haters...They are just
angry because the truth you speak
contradicts the lie they live.
DR STEVE MARABOLI

No, this chapter isn't about revenge, bitterness and other evil things like that. It's about empowering you. Because, to be frank, people are fuckwits, and they *will* criticise what you do, say or are. In fact, the more successful and awesome you become, the more haters you attract.

But this chapter will show why that's OK. It's OK to be hated, 'cause that's when you know what you are doing is making the haters uncomfortable. It highlights to them their mediocre life, health and relationships.

So you have to be smart and use this to improve yourself. Show 'em what you're capable of. There's no better motivation than a will to show someone who thought you were scum that actually you're an awesome fucking successful machine. And hot as balls (if that gets you going).

Let's take a little trip down memory lane...

A teenage boy's mind, when the hormones kick in, tends to go from 'girls are rubbish' to 'girls are awesome'. (Or boys, or whatever you are into. Essentially I am guessing it's all the same.).

Anyway, I remember camping in a friend's back garden (yeah, we were that cool – we even used the microwave in the house) with, among others, a young lady I'd had my eye on for a while. In fact, I had quite the crush.

Just imagine. Little ole Dan, all smitten!

OK, bad imagery, sorry.

Anyway, although in my teens, I was hardly what you would call blessed in the looks department, with some amazingly afro-esque hair, double train track braces, and drought and famine resistant – aka, fat (thank you, Homer Simpson, for that analogy). But we had got on quite well during the course of the evening, and I actually thought I was in with a chance.

BE SPITEFUL

The boys were in one tent, and the girls were in the other. We were chatting nonsense, and even though we had settled down for the night, I had consumed some cider and really needed to pee. I got out of the tent, and just as I walked past the girls' tent, I heard my name.

I was tempted to listen in. So I did.

I remember it as clearly as if it was yesterday.

'I would definitely go out with Dan, he's lovely. It's just a shame he is so fat.'

Ha! Looking back, with all those hormones racing through me, I can almost hear my little heart audibly breaking. Bless!

So, apart from going to bed with my dreams in tatters, I lay there thinking, I'll show you. The next day I copied what my parents did and started the day with coffee – that's it. I threw my lunch away, only ate dinner and then ran six miles every day over the hilly coastline in the West Country where I come from.

Yes, I know now that is perhaps the worst possible way to lose weight – that's not for discussion here – but in four or five months I'd dropped from around 15 stone to just under 10 stone. Bearing in mind I am, give or take, 6ft tall, I looked like I was made of wire hangers and elastic bands.

Sexy, eh?

But although I looked quite ill, I had dropped all of the fat that had turned the young lady off (as well as pretty much any muscle). I never did go out with her; the whole experience really put me off her. I saw her a few years ago and time hasn't been kind...ha! Sorry, that was a proper bitchy moment.

This was the first, but very much not the last, time I have harnessed the power of spite to not only achieve, but smash my goals into pieces. It may sound like a really negative emotion to harbour, and if you do it the wrong way, it can make you a bitter and twisted fuck, but if you are going to do your own thing – whether that be with your business, your life, your relationships or whatever area you are trying to improve – some people are going to piss on your parade. It's going to happen, so expect it. And if it hasn't happened yet – oh, it's coming.

I don't know what it is with some people, but they just want to keep you down at their level and don't want you to succeed in your endeavours. I have heard people say this is because when you achieve success, it's a reflection of what they *haven't* achieved.

I agree with that to a degree.

Equally, I think some people are dicks.

A great analogy I heard was that some people want to tear down your castle so it's no bigger than theirs or anyone else's, while other people want to build the highest castle in the land to inspire others to do the same. I may have utterly fucked that up, and I Googled it for ages, but fuck it – you get the drift.

Some people don't want you to succeed for whatever reason. It's sad, but they don't want you to grow and will do all manner of things to sabotage you.

Why? Because it makes them feel safe. You making a go of your life actually puts their shitty life on show. Which is fucking scary as hell to them. So they try to keep you at or below their level.

If it's business, they will tell you that your product/service won't work, you don't have the talent for it, no one wants it or simply badmouth you.

If it's your health or fitness, they will tempt you with junk food, encourage you to go drinking, tell you that you will always be fat/skinny/unfit/weak.

If it's relationships, you could hear things like 'You will never get anyone better'; 'You don't deserve that person'; 'You would be a crap mum/dad'.

Bastards, eh?

And, because I am really enjoying the F-bombs in this one – it's quite an emotionally charged topic for me – to those people I say, 'Fuck. You.'.

And you must do the same.

Take note, though, sometimes what they are saying may have a grain of truth in it. In my case, when I was a kid, I was – well, fat! You don't have to take on board anyone's opinion. It's your life, and what you choose to do with your life is up to you. But, as always, keep your antennae up for the tiny truth you may need to hear from time to time. Then, you take that truth and prove the haters wrong.

I'll tell you now, there is no greater feeling than proving someone wrong, but there is a right way and a wrong way to do it, which I'll outline shortly.

These are some of the things I have been told I would never be able to do, followed by what I achieved in spite of the naysayers:

'You will never be big or strong.' I got up to 17 stone of mainly muscle, could squat and deadlift 240kg+, and had 32inch thighs of doom!

'You will never be successful.' I made it to the six-figure mark in three different industries, am on target for a seven-figure year (may already have done so by the time you read this, fingers crossed!), have multiple offline and online businesses, and it keeps growing.

'You will never have a good looking woman in your life.' (Yep, I told you I had some bastards in my past). Well, I've dated a world class dancer, models, a few actresses and women who, to all intents and purposes, are *waaaay* out of my league. Oh, and they were cool as fuck and funny as balls too. Not all about looks, you vain bugger, ha!

So a lot of the successes in my life have been born out of people telling me that I can't do something. Hence I love spite, but I am very careful *never* to rub it in anyone's face. I simply let my actions do the talking.

You don't need to make a big deal about it. You don't need to show off. You don't need to ring people up and tell them what you have done. Mainly because people are so preoccupied with their own shit, they often don't remember putting you down, or if they do, they will still tell you what you've achieved is not good enough anyway.

So if someone tells you that you can't do something, you simply need to make a mental note of it, figure out how you can prove them wrong, and – I'm sure you are noticing a theme now – go and do it. Then sit back, smile inwardly and enjoy the fruits of your labour. While they burn with envy or jealousy.

Burn, burn, burn.

Oh, and by the way, those fruits taste fucking good...

BE SPITEFUL (PROVE 'EM WRONG) TO DO/ACTION STEPS

What to do if somebody tells you that you can't do something.
You simply need to make a mental note of it, figure out how you can prove them wrong and go do it. Then sit back, relax and smile. Enjoy the fruits of your labour.

Get it into your head that people will criticise and hate you.
There really is no better motivation than a will to prove someone wrong. You have to understand that if you're going to do your own thing, whatever part of your life it's in, some people are going to piss on your parade and try to drag you down. It's your job to realise that they are most likely holding up a mirror and presenting their own insecurities on to you because they are scared of you succeeding.

Keep your antennae up. You want to be listening out for the tiny pieces of truth you may need to hear from time to time. Be wary of what others say to you and what you feel in your life. But sometimes what people are saying may have a grain of truth in it.

There is no greater feeling than proving someone wrong. Spite is awesome. But be very careful never to rub it in anyone's face. Let your actions do the talking. There's no need to show off.

8

BE PRODUCTIVE

Focus on being productive instead of busy.
TIM FERRIS

Doing work for work's sake is fucking stupid. There, I said it.

This chapter will outline the strategies I've used to get to where I am today.

You can't get to this stage (honestly) without being super productive with your time. Otherwise you'll burn out, lose motivation, give up and head back to the J.O.B with your tail between your legs. And again, there is nothing wrong with having a job. Just if you're doing one that sucks – I feel for you. I won't let that happen. You're here to make your life awesome, so let's give you the productivity recipe that you need. And it's one that I've used for myself too.

And if you have been in my Facebook group ('Coffee With Dan') long enough, you'll know that I run by the philosophy of 'getting shit done'. Heck, I even had shirts printed with that statement on, and a lot of CWD loons actually bought them too (with all the proceeds going to charity).

It's safe to say this is the chapter I'll excel in. Hence it's the longest of them all. But what that means is you'll learn all the nuggets of mine to start implementing in your life too.

So grab a coffee, and let's crack on.

This is the cornerstone of my philosophy: being productive. Or, more in my parlance, getting shit done. It is a premise that I have built my career on, and quite frankly I know no other way.

This is where – for once – I will be closed-minded.

Why?

Because it fucking works! I'm taking all the stuff I've done to get where I am and dumping it on the pages of this book just for you.

You're welcome.

So, instead of looking up to the sky for answers from the universe, twatting around with vision boards, or simply hoping one day good shit will happen, I finally *made* shit happen. No chakras and all that bull involved. (But, like I said, if that's working for you, you keep reaching for the rainbow, OK?)

As I mentioned earlier, Old Dan used to have a rather tenacious drinking hobby. On a hungover Tuesday(!) morning, I realised that, although I was doing pretty well at what I was doing (consulting, coaching and copywriting at the time), I could do so much more if I was a little more structured, disciplined and productive. But, as I can be a bit of a charmer, I had a knack of talking myself *out* of doing the work (it's perfectly normal to talk to yourself, I think…), so I realised if I couldn't hold myself accountable, I needed to get others to do it with me.

I surrounded myself with these others, committed to certain actions and, in essence, took charge of the group of folks so that I *had* to show up every day. Because I was the leader. I couldn't let the side down by not showing up.

It started when I put a post up on Facebook. I simply said I was going to be doing an accountability group for anyone who was interested. I then (something I learned from an Australian gentlemen called James Schramko) put up an accountability post at 9am and 3pm as they were my optimal times. The goal was for people to commit to doing two blocks of two hours a day to post up what they intended to do, and then what they'd actually done. I also said I would try and teach them, from time to time, some of the stuff I had learned about sales, marketing, copywriting, creating digital products, networking and so forth.

I had hoped for fifteen–twenty people. As of writing that was less than a year ago. Right now, the group stands at over 4,000, with 700+ people waiting to be admitted.

The group is called 'Coffee With Dan'. The idea was to create a virtual coffee shop co-working environment.

Mind blowing, right? I mean, really. What. The. Fuck.

So, the group was based around the themes of getting shit done, doing the work, productivity, serving your tribe and having some fun (entrepreneurs can be so bloody boring at times). I will share more on this in a later chapter, but if you want to get more shit done, surround yourself with people who equally want to get shit done.

Again, I know it's simple, but hardly anyone does it.

I digress.

As a result, I've become quite an expert in what makes *me* productive. Now a lot of my clients and 'Coffee With Dan' members have adopted some, or all, of my ideas. And, I hasten to add, they were patchworked together from books, trainings, anecdotal observations and people smarter than me – I will give them due credit at the back of the book. These are things I have tried, adapted and put myself through.

Use these and you'll be laughing, because they fucking work. Don't try and reinvent the wheel.

I mentioned earlier that you should factor in stuff like family time, fun, exercise, education, and so forth *before* you plan your week in a business capacity. This is one of the biggest breakthroughs I have had, and I owe it all to a book called *The 12 Week Year* by Brian Moran and Michael Lennington, because that is where I first got the idea. I suggest you go and buy it – it's brilliant. But my version is, like anything I do, far simpler, because I'm a simpleton.

This is what I do. First, I block out all the stuff that's important to me, so that's fitness, personal development/education, 'nothing time' (I literally schedule an hour a day for nothing. Sometimes I nap, go for a walk, piss around online – whatever I feel like), time with my family, film night, train journeys to nowhere (I'll explain this genius later) and so forth.

Then I put in time at the start of my week to have a team meeting and get everything planned. This is usually on a Monday, and I have the heads of each of my businesses in on the call, as well as any team members who want to dive in. I then schedule a much shorter call at the end of the week, which is far less formal, where we review how the week has gone against what we planned to do. I also tend to make filthy jokes and say terrible things.

After this, I always have a massage of some form. Sounds odd, but I learned this from people smarter than me. It serves a few key purposes: it not only signals the official end of the week (I still work at weekends, but only on stuff I want to do), it also helps with my stress levels. That, and I have royally fucked my body up with rugby, lifting stupidly heavy things and falling over drunk in the past.

Plum.

Regardless, it's my way of telling my body, 'I'm done for the week'.

Each week, I factor in either a whole or half day, depending on how busy I am, to simply go and have fun. I never plan it. I just ensure it is blocked off in my diary, and I go adventuring. It's good for the soul. I often tend to find myself in an aquarium or an arcade, or jet skiing or roaming round a museum. Thirty-five-year-old man-child doesn't do it justice, really...

Only after all of the above have been slotted into my diary do I put in work slots, coaching calls, new business development, 'dentist appointments', content creation and meetings.

It's utterly contradictory to how most people work but, once you try it, you won't turn back. If you want more of the reasons why it works then go and buy *The 12 Week Year*. The authors are smarter than me.

But the gist is: you work better and are more productive in short bursts than long stretched out blocks.

Now we come on to some 'Dan-isms' and weird things I do that work. These things might seem quite odd, but I have tested them on myself first, as well as willing (and sometimes unwilling) clients. Try them, and let me know how they go for you.

MY SUNDAY BRAIN DUMP AND 3-5 SYSTEM

There's a story behind how this system came about and I'd like to share it with you.

As I'm a simpleton, I'd get rather frustrated and overwhelmed with all the shit in my head that equated to things I had to do. So I decided to do a brain dump.

This took me, at the time, two hours and resulted in 169 things to do.

Safe to say, I did none of them.

That list was so utterly mammoth and daunting, I thought, fuck it, I'm never going to get that done, and put the thing in the bin. This is what most people do. And this is why most people remain overworked, bitter fuckwits.

You, my friend, are not a fuckwit.

I spoke to a personal training client I had at the time. Back then I was still doing fortyish hours a week of PT, was head of special projects (lol) for a massive gym chain, doing the whole 'iamthefitnesscopywriter' thing and trying to get my own facility up and running.

Needless to say, I was busy as fuck.

This chap happens to be one of the most successful people in town, and had achieved everything he'd set out to achieve when he was still in his twenties. He has the best house in the area (it really is; it's *sick*), a tall blonde model-esque wife (and she is lovely), his own business (and it's the best in the world at what it does) and is a millionaire (safe to say he'd have that covered).

He taught me what he had been using, Monday to Friday, for twenty+ years – and as a direct result he had not only removed a metric shit-tonne of stress and ball ache from his life, he was massively productive. Looking back now, it looks so simple – and it is.

He said, 'Every day I write a list. That list has no less than three and no more than five important things that I need to do for my business. That, Dan, is all I do.'

Eh? Three–five things? Surely not!

Well, one thing I have learned: when someone is more successful than you in anything, don't argue. Just shut up and do as you're told. So I did.

I came up with a ranking system, 1, 2 or 3:

1. = super important, business critical, time/deadline bound, makes money, or only I can do it.
2. = important, but doesn't need to be done now: exploratory business meetings, interview/podcasts/guest content – things that need my input, but a team member could handle.
3. = not time bound, not critical, someone else could do it, whimsical business ideas, 'busy fool' work.

I then do the brain dump. I find it easier to do this on a laptop and print it out, but writing it out is fine as well. Basically, I let out all the tasks and dump them on to paper, rank the brain dump with the 1, 2, 3 system as above, then go through, highlight all the 1s, take my diary and put no less than three and no more than five things to do in each day from Monday to Friday. If I have space, I'll put in some of the 2s and maybe the odd 3 as well, but that, in essence, is it.

Now bear this in mind: really analyse the tasks and see which category they fit in. don't just put a 1 next to something which can actually be a 2 or even a 3. Be ruthless and stick to the system.

Another area that you might find works for you is themes. I can't switch very easily from a new business call to a coaching call or writing content. It takes me a while to get out of one mindset and into another, so what I do is this (and you can make your own versions up depending on what you do):

- Monday – planning
- Tuesday – coaching
- Wednesday – meetings (and generally a half day)
- Thursday – copy and content creation
- Friday – new business development and marketing
- Saturday – social media and emails
- Sunday – free-balling. Whatever I want as a rule.

That way, I don't have to flip between one thing and another, and I'm conscientious about putting the right 1s on the right days.

The great thing is, it makes your time very precious, and you know exactly where you stand if you need to slot something or someone in. I used to beat myself up if I didn't do my full five things. If I do – great, but as long as I do the minimum three my business continues to grow.

As for the 2s and 3s – well, if someone wants you to do something, and they're not a paying client (who always should come first) or an influencer or someone looking to work with you, if it's *really* important, they will chase you.

I know that sounds bad, but as someone who lived to please people, I ended up being a 'busy fool'. In other words, it looked like I was doing a lot of work, but in reality I was kidding myself. Being busy is not the same as being productive. As I said earlier, a degree of being selfish with your time, and being honest about what you are actually doing, will do wonders for you.

Trust me. If someone chases you, they want you. If they don't? Well, their task wasn't that important in the first place, so no harm done.

This is especially true as you get more and more successful and/or well-known.

THE DENTIST APPOINTMENT

This was taught to me by a chap called John Logar. And I totally believe this is where most people fuck up.

A business without sales is just ego masturbation. Sure you can say you have a business, but without sales, you have nothing.

Equally, I have found – as I have done this myself – businesses, especially in the early stages, go through a 'feast and famine' cycle. You do loads of marketing and calls and advertising when you start, then all of a sudden you have all these clients to serve. Then, when you have finished with them, you think, shit, I need more clients!

Happens every day.

Which is why I love the dentist appointment philosophy. Simply put in, Monday to Friday, one hour for a dental appointment. When you go to the dentist you usually allow for an hour, right? Especially if you are having work done. Same here, except this time the dentist appointment is one hour, every day, of new business development. That, and nothing else is scheduled for that hour. The hour is taken.

Now, many of you won't do this. Because not many people like sales or selling. For starters, you need to get over that shit! Cheesy, hardcore, 'buy my shit' sales – yes, that is dire. But if you have a product or service that helps people, you genuinely believe in it *and* it works, then it is your duty to sell that product. (I think this is a Dan Kennedy thing – either way, go buy all his books, now!) If you don't sell that product and it can help them, you are a fuckin' plum.

Er, what?

Yes, that's right – your duty. Plum.

If you have something that can help someone, take them out of whatever pain they are in, make them feel good, add value to their life, make them money – whatever – why the fuck would you not want to sell it to them? You are being a selfish dick not giving it to them, and getting them to feel better.

See? It's all a matter of perspective.

Anyway, I'm getting off topic. One hour of new business a day, every day – *especially* when you don't need it – means you have a consistent deal flow and pipeline of prospects.

Don't question, just do it.

THE TRAIN RIDE TO NOWHERE (AKA THE SOCIALLY AWKWARD SITUATION)

I like trains.

I used to hate them when I had to commute, but now I think they are awesome. I get so much work done on them. I think most people, when they get on public transport, have their own stuff to deal with, and as a result they want to be left alone.

I love this.

If I have to crank out a stack of work, I plan a trip to somewhere around two hours away – with no changes – and make sure I book a table seat. I commit to two hours of extremely focused work, get off the train – have lunch, go shopping, potter around – then get back on the train home for another two hours of extremely focused work.

By doing this, I end up being super productive and doing (as I know I only have two hours each way) more than a day's work in four hours. Give it a punt if you need to get shit done in a hurry. It's awesome.

ONE BAG PHILOSOPHY

I have a lot of time for people who serve their country. Whether you agree with it or not, they do a tough job that I don't think I could do, and they do it well.

A good friend of mine once told me how he lived while in the military. Essentially he had everything he needed in one bag. If he needed to get the fuck out of dodge, the bag was ready to roll.

Now, I don't tend to find myself in combat situations, but I did, at one point, realise I had accumulated so much crap over the years that the idea of moving out filled me with dread.

I realised there were lots of clothes, gadgets, books – things that I had either never used or they'd been at the bottom of a drawer or cupboard for so long that I didn't even know I had them.

It was an easy fix. If I hadn't used something in the last six months, it went to the charity shop. As a result I have far less stuff I don't need. All I have is what I actually use, which gives me a whole lot of freedom.

It lifts a burden off your mind. The less clutter there is around you, the less cluttered your mind is.

I do the same when I travel. I travel internationally, sometimes for a month at a time, with carry on only. When I'm in the States it can be a touch tricky as the weather can go from basking sunshine to frozen icy madness. But with a week's worth of underwear, some T-shirts, smart and casual jeans, a decent pair of shoes, some quick-dry gym kit and portable versions of everything, I can travel the world, wash as I go, and be completely free.

It's massively liberating. That, and you don't have to wait for your luggage, which is amazing! I promise you that you *don't* need as much shit as you pack. Really. I'm a fucking pro at this now.

BLAST AND CRUISE

I got this idea from a humongous man who was talking about the spectacular levels of steroids he took to look, quite frankly, like he was made of footballs. Essentially, he would take all the drugs for three months, become a giant of a man, then drop his dose for three months to maintain.

I have no idea if there is any scientific basis for this, but I loved the name, and I loved the concept. So leaning again on the *12 Week Year* philosophy, I 'Danified' it and came up with this:

Ninety days of bat shit crazy new business development, recruiting team members,– balls to the wall for the entire time. Do lots of work.

Ninety days of chilled maintenance, putting systems and staff in place to handle volume of work, serve clients, getting feedback, refining process. Do less work and enjoy life.

When I launch a new business venture I give it exactly ninety days to work. If it is not profitable, fun, takes up too much of my time or pisses me off, I tank it. Please note this is *not* for everyone! It just works well for me. I have hung on to ventures before that I should have let go a lot earlier. That and the hard deadline really focuses me.

REPEAT, REPEAT, REPEAT

If I need to crank work out, get shit done or focus for extended periods, I find a song that gets me in the right mood (whether that mood be creative or furious action). Put it on repeat. Listen to it over and over again until the work is done.

I have no idea why this works, but my hunch is that the song occupies the part of my brain that goes 1,000 miles an hour and helps it to switch off. Anyway, I'm pretty damn far away from being a neuroscientist, but I know it works for me and lots of other folk who have tried it.

THE ROUTINE OF DAN

I get asked a lot about what my routine is. People seem to love the concept of the 'power hour' – that first hour of the day (there are quite a few books on this).

As always, I have my own version, a lot simpler and more manageable. I'm going to give you my morning routine, and my evening routine as that sets up the next morning routine.

Feel free to shamelessly steal and integrate this into your own life.

Morning routine. Unless I have a meeting or somewhere to be, I don't set an alarm. When my body wakes me up, that's when I get up. Some days I need a lot of sleep/recovery. Some days I am wide awake after four hours. Ever since I stopped obsessing about my sleep (because I am quite shit at it as a rule) I feel amazing most days.

My brain is smarter than me; I let it handle things.

If I do need to wake up, I use an old-school wind-up alarm clock.

Really.

Next, and I learned this from Ben Settle, the first part of my day I am massively selfish with. It's mine. All mine...

You can't have it!

Since I have done this my mood and general love for what I do have increased considerably. Once I feel human, I'll go make a coffee, sit on my balcony and simply do two minutes of controlled breathing.

I can't meditate for shit. In fact, you have more chance of catching me clean-shaven than sitting cross-legged, eyes shut, in some fucking lotus position or whatever.

So I use an App that I breathe in and out to. (Honestly now, don't start emailing me about which App. Any will do.) It works, sorts my head out, and I've been less stressed since I started doing it.

Like many things in life, two minutes, job done – ha! (Sorry, ladies.)

Next, I read. Now I have three books on the go at all times. As I mentioned earlier, I used to beat myself up over having all the books and not reading them. Now? I pick the most suitable three and read one–two chapters of each of them every day. For me, a combination of an autobiography, a business/marketing/mindset book and some easy, fun-to-read fiction works well.

Then I'll watch some stand-up comedy, some 'grown-up cartoons', fuck around on the Xbox or do something that makes me equally happy.

Why?

Well, we all have those days when we see an email or message and it pisses us right off. By putting myself in an awesome mood first thing, I find I'm nowhere near as bothered if someone gets on my tits or annoys me.

What I haven't mentioned so far is what I do with my phone. One thing I *don't* do is look at it till at least mid–late morning. It's too easy to let that little fucker run your life – I know it has mine more than once – and in today's modern world we can all be reached so easily. I've realised that most of the stuff you get on email and in various inboxes is rarely life or death. So don't let that little digital prick tell you what to do.

I'll explain why in my evening routine, but I would suggest you give your mobile number only to people like family, partner, kids and close friends.

Evening routine. A little shorter this time, but equally important. For starters – make sure you don't have any calls or work stuff unless it's hyper critical in the last two hours of your day. Yes, there are times when you have to go balls/ovaries deep – but try and keep the last few hours of your day to yourself.

If I am working, although I look like a massive tool, I wear funky orange glasses that block UV light. The blue light that is emitted from *everything* fucks up our natural rhythms, and these bad boys block that blue light so my brain senses sleepy time soon.

Oh, on that matter, make sure you get *anything* that emits a blue light out of your bedroom. Get some heavy-arsed blackout blinds, and keep your room a little cold.

I was taught all this by a genius called Ari Meisel. He has an amazing productivity App (called 'Peak Time') and a virtual assistant service that is fucking awesome. Check him out.

Again, I won't go into detail (we're already overwhelmed with info). Just do it. It works. You will thank me when you actually get a good night's sleep.

In those last two hours, I turn *all* notifications off (except text and calls as those will be from peeps I want to be able to reach me if they need to). Really, if something's that important, others will find a way to get hold of me, but as a rule, if I get a message that late, it can wait.

Remember whose life it is, OK?

The last few hours of the day are for you to chill. If you want to Netflix binge for a few hours, watch mindless TV, blow up zombies online or do something more refined like reading or listening to music, no one has the right to steal that time from you.

You work bloody hard enough all day; this time is for you. Be selfish with it.

Then, the final piece of the puzzle is: take that phone, take the charging cable and leave the little bastard in another room. Takes a bit of discipline, but again trust me on this. Most people are slaves to their phones. Your bedroom should be reserved for two things.

Sleeping and sex.

Or maybe building a pillow fort. That is also acceptable.

BE PRODUCTIVE TO DO/ACTION STEPS

How to set your week up for success (the 3–5 system). Spend some time (I do this Sunday evening) writing down everything on paper that you want to get done. Empty your head of *everything*. Once you've got a list of things to do, you're going to want to rank them 1, 2 or 3.

1. – super important
2. – important, but doesn't need to be done immediately
3. – not time bound or critical

Highlight all the 1s and build out your diary, starting with the most important tasks. No less than three, no more than five things to do per day. If you have space, start adding 2s and 3s to your days.

The dentist appointment. Aka simply one hour every day to work on new business development. Find one hour slots in your day when you can focus and let the creative side of you come out.

Take a train ride to nowhere. This is bloody brilliant. If you've got a stack of work to crank out and you need a focused place to do it, plan a trip somewhere around two hours away with no changes. Oh, and by the way, make sure you book a table seat. Commit to two hours of extremely focused work. Get off the train, go have fun, have lunch, potter around, and then return for another two hours of focused work on the way home.

My one bag philosophy. If you want to lift a heavy burden off yourself, have less clutter and relax your mind. Do this. If you're travelling, take just as much as you need and make sure it fits in only one small bag (a carry on size).

Repeat, repeat, repeat. Find a song that gets you in the right mood. Whack that on repeat. Listen to it over and over again until the work is done. This alone helps me switch off from trying to run at 1,000 miles an hour.

The first hour (it's all yours). Be selfish with the first hour of your day. Don't fuck around on Facebook or check your emails. Get yourself in the right frame of mind to start the day. By doing this you're going to be in a more focused mood to get shit done during the day. Read a book, or watch some stand-up comedy – whatever floats your boat.

9

BE AROUND LIKEMINDED PEOPLE

Who you hang out with determines what you dream about and what you collide with. And the collisions and the dreams lead to your changes. And the changes are what you become. Change the outcome by changing your circle.

SETH GODIN

Let me explain. Normal people around you won't have a clue what you are doing. Nor will they understand jack shit about what you're going through on this journey of entrepreneurialism and awesomeness.

So it's important to surround yourself with likeminded people – those who are not only on the same journey as you, but some who are further along the line or maybe slightly behind you.

The key is they should have similar goals, ambitions and values to you.

There's no point hanging round lazy fucking people who are unhappy with their soul-sucking jobs (and refuse to do anything about it), only waiting until the weekend to numb their senses partying until 4am and wasting the money they just spent sixty+ hours in the week earning. That or they sit in front of the TV, slowly letting their life slip by. They then do the same again the following week.

No aim, no game.

This concept of surrounding myself with my kinda people has actually accelerated my success tenfold. And I implore you to take note and implement this chapter like a mofo.

So let's crack on...

Before we begin, I'd just like to say that coaches and mentors are not magic bullets. If you want results, you, and only you, have to do the work. Nobody can do it for you. I see people hiring good coaches (shit ones are, well – shit) then whining as things don't work out for them. Often these people did none of the work and are simply looking for someone to blame.

But I digress.

BE AROUND LIKEMINDED PEOPLE

This topic – again – may seem simple, but it actually takes a bit of effort and a bit of trial and error to get right.

But when you do? It can be transformational to the point you will kick yourself for not doing it sooner.

I want you to get the concept of being around people just like you and people you want to be like in your head. I did this with a combination of Facebook groups (and when I couldn't find one that really fitted me, I made my own: 'Coffee With Dan'), masterminds, events, seminars, coaches and mentors. All, I believe, are important for your growth as a person.

I'm going to address one thing right off the bat. You may have already experienced this, or maybe you're yet to do so, but as you get better at what you do and more driven to achieve your goals, you are going to lose friends. Full stop.

Now, this is coming from someone who identifies himself as a people pleaser. I've been told I suffer from something called 'Superman syndrome'. In other words, I want to help and/or save everyone.

But realistically? I can't. It's just not possible.

When you start to make changes and good shit happens for you, you will naturally find your circle of friends will evolve. And it will include more people who are like you, or on a similar mission.

You know that saying, that you are the sum of the five people you tend to spend the most time with? It rings true. I love my friends. And those I grew up with, met at university or picked up along the way I cherish.

But the people I spend the most time with tend to be as driven and ambitious as me. Of course, I make time for my mates. It would make me an utter scumbag if I dropped them.

Some people won't get what you are doing, and simply think it's odd, and that's OK. That's their right. But flip the coin and there are others who will down right want to keep you unsuccessful. Safe to say you'll soon see their true colours emerge.

People you may have looked up to, respected, and classed as friends turn on you. It's sad, but it happens. It doesn't make you or them bad people; it's just the way it is. As I mentioned earlier in the book, some people are simply going to resent your ambition or success. Because it highlights their ambitiousness, or lack of it.

It hurts – really it does – and I hope it doesn't happen to you. But I need you to be ready for it, 'cause it can cripple you if they had been really close friends.

I have spoken to many people about this – seems to be a fact of life when you start to make it.

I'm just giving you a heads up.

Right, positive and useful shit now!

So, I'm sure we agree that surrounding yourself with people on a similar mission to you is a good thing. But how do you find them? Well, here are a few ideas to get you started.

Facebook groups and forums. This is a great low/no cost option and is where I advise everyone to start. Find a group that fits your ethos, filled with people like you, and join in.

I have noticed with my own group there are a lot of 'lurkers' who read but never interact. I haven't actually met a lurker who makes big changes in their life. Mainly because they don't get involved, and that tends to translate into real life as well.

But equally there are a lot more action takers who fully interact and make the group what it is. Simply awesome. Don't be a lurker; become one of the action takers.

If you join a group, forum or community, maybe spend a little while seeing who is in charge, who the major players are, understanding the lingo and how it works – then dive in! Introduce yourself, contribute, add value (yes, no matter how new you are to whatever it is you're doing, you have value).

Couple of things, though. Don't be too keen. We all know that person who is too into it. Enthusiasm is great, but don't make people want to avoid you by being too full on. Play it cool.

Add value before you take. Don't be afraid to ask for help, pertinent questions or join in on conversations. Simply put, I have found being a useful member of a community before asking for anything goes a long way.

Give before you expect to get.

And don't spam or pitch. That's a dick move.

In person events and seminars. These are great for meeting other folks like you. Personally I find the paid ones better, which is directly in line with my 'pay to play' philosophy which I will go into in more depth later. It's also an opportunity to connect with influencers and other industry leaders on a personal level.

So, a good thing, then.

Want a tip? Let's just say you have a service – and let's say that service has an audience. Might be worth popping along, right?

This is what I did when I launched my fitness copywriting business.

Instead of going to events with other copywriters, I went to events for fitness professionals. Then through organic conversations and networking (ugh, I *hate* that word) I picked up a shit-tonne of business with zero pitching or effort.

I did the same when I was a headhunter. I went to the industry events of my niche and chatted to people. When they invariably asked what I did, I told them, and as a result picked up a stack of clients.

Sometimes it's not people but places that inspire you to get shit done and show you what your life could be like.

Brilliantly, you can do this for free or, at most, the price of a cup of coffee. If you are looking to increase your wealth, sometimes being in places where wealth *is* can inspire you. I often go to fancy-as-fuck hotels and have a coffee in the lobby or bar and work for an hour or two. I can't quite explain the mechanism, but being around success and wealth, if that's your thing, is pretty bloody inspiring. Plus, it's really good fun to try and blag your way into fancy places. It has become somewhat of a hobby of mine to see where I can get into.

I have heard of people taking luxury cars for a test drive, hanging out in the bars at fancy events (and if you are skint this is a great way to meet people and connect as all the best stuff is done at the bar, not in the main room), or buying passes to the executive airport lounge just to experience it.

Once you have done it a few times, it's weird – it kinda becomes normal and not quite as amazing as you think. That in itself is a great mindset switch and I encourage you to try it as often as you can. Because if you want it badly enough, you can get it. I didn't think I could for a long time – now I can. But brilliantly, now I can, I don't really want it.

What a dick, eh?

Coaches and mentors. I attribute a huge part of my success wholly to having coaching and mentors.

But, I believe there is a difference between a coach and a mentor.

I've found that coaches are extremely useful for up-levelling a skill, helping you get through a particular period in your growth, or providing a sounding board and subsequent advice for what you are doing.

A mentor is someone who has a '30,000ft view' of you, your business, your life and your overall growth as a person. I've found coaches useful for three–six month stints. Enough for me to get through the hump or master/develop the skill I was trying to develop. When it comes to mentors, I believe they should be with you for one year+ as they have a longer term vision, extensive experience and might need to guide you through areas that are somewhat tricky.

I want to make one thing clear, though: no one, and I mean no one, makes it on their own.

Every successful person I have met has had people around them who have offered guidance, support or, in my case, a metaphorical 'slap down' (I get very excited and want to do all the things). If you think you can make it on your own, my response is simple.

You won't.

So, as well as potentially upgrading your friends to include more people like you and getting among your peers, investing in coaches and mentors is, in my opinion, crucial.

No money?

Well don't let that stop you. When it comes to people teaching you their skills for free in a coaching capacity, that's solely going to be down to whether you can offer them something of value in return. Maybe you can do some grunt work or help them in some way, or perhaps you can give them a percentage of what you generate – or perhaps you are just likeable as shit!

Either way, it will be up to you to do your best.

When it comes to mentors, I have had great success with people who do not in any way advertise themselves as such. They could be a successful businessperson in your local community, or maybe someone you have seen online and you really identify with who is doing what you would like to be doing. You have *nothing* to lose by asking. Write them a letter. A real one if possible. Trust me, this works, and effort goes a *long* way.

In this letter, outline your thoughts and feelings about why they would make a good mentor. Make them an offer. It could be dinner, or to travel to see them. Be creative – what can you offer to them in return?

If you get nervous about doing this, I want to tell you a story from my recruitment days. I was due to interview an industry titan as a mere twenty-one-year-old. He was in his early forties, slick, handsome as fuck, had all the monies and was industry-wide renowned as the best in the business.

He rolled up in a red Ferrari.

As I introduced myself and sat him down, I was clearly nervous. It would have been easy for him to dominate the meeting, bully me into doing what he wanted business-wise and generally make me his bitch.

But he didn't.

He said, 'Dan, I can tell you are nervous, but I want you to realise I'm a guy, like you. Just older, and a bit more successful. If this helps, I want to tell you something that my first boss told me. He said that everyone sits down to take a shit.'

Then he said, 'Imagine me taking a shit.'

Ridiculous image, isn't it?

I, of course, pissed myself laughing, but it's stuck with me ever since. We're all human, all have the same wants, needs, and desires, and we all shit. Next time you meet someone who you think is a player – just remember that.

I couldn't give a toss if someone has no money or a golden space yacht – I treat everyone the same. I'm respectful, of course, but they are not better than me, and I am not better than them. I might be a bit further ahead, or vice versa. It doesn't matter.

Treat people as you want to be treated. No one is special. They are just a person, and if they make you feel like crap, fuck 'em off. They aren't worth knowing in the first place.

Pay to play. I have touched on this before.

One thing I have realised is that once you invest in someone, they take you more seriously. It's all too easy to shoot someone a message asking to pick their brains without thinking how that makes you look. If you want people to value your time and abilities, it starts with you valuing (and being prepared to pay for) theirs.

One thing I learned early on is that if you want someone's attention or time, you pay. It's that simple. Every time I made a few quid, I would immediately reinvest what I had spare in coaches and mentors – they're that powerful. Because not only do you get their wisdom and skills as they've done it before you, but if they are good, you get access to their network too. They can make introductions, create opportunities and deals that would take you ages to crack.

Like anything, though, don't take the piss. But really, this is an area you should invest in and, like I said, it doesn't always have to be about money. Learn what value you can add then pitch away to your heart's content.

This may all seem a bit nuts, especially if you are from a small town like me. But it's so important to get out of your comfort zone, connect with people who are on the same path as you, spend actual time in person to cultivate and develop relationships that can last a lifetime and provide crucial support when you need it the most.

Really, don't overlook this part. Find a mentor. Get coaches. Make some new friends and crack the fuck on!

BE AROUND LIKEMINDED PEOPLE TO DO/ACTION STEPS

Surround yourself with likeminded people. When I say this, I don't just mean the ones you look up to, but some who are further along the line or maybe slightly behind you. Find a group that fits your ethos (Facebook is a good place to start). Join groups and start adding *value*. Don't be a lurker – you know, the one who sits at the back, reads and never interacts. Boring as balls. Be active in the group and introduce yourself.

Fish where the fish are. I did this with my copywriting business and you could say it worked out pretty well. Instead of going to events that other copywriters attend, go to events *your* audience is going to. Then through organic conversations you can build quality relationships. It's not a pitch fest.

Put yourself in a place to win. Sometimes it's not people but places that inspire you to get shit done. Start living and going to the places you want in your lifestyle. This is what your life *could* look like.

Start paying to play. Stop asking to pick people's brains and start investing in people. Invest your time and maybe a little bit of money, showing that you respect their time and abilities. They'll teach you the skills you want to learn as well as opening you up to their network – this is massive. It is *that* powerful. They will be able to introduce you and create opportunities. That's why it's so important you get out of your little bubble of comfort and start connecting with people. Meet people face to face and get the hell off Facebook.

10

BE RELENTLESS

You must be passionate, you must dedicate yourself,
and you must be relentless in the pursuit of your
goals. If you do, you will be successful.
STEVE GARVEY

If you think that becoming successful is a piece of pie, you are deluded, my friend. It takes balls/ovaries. Because it includes failure, pain, hard work and fucking relentlessness.

Oh, and a healthy dose of 'stick-to-it-iveness'.

You'll have to be disciplined to make the changes, and trust me, that's where most people fail. Miserably.

They think they'll get some silver bullet of info from a book or course which will make them millions overnight. The truth is much more boring and unsexy than that.

It's being consistent, working hard, and being relentless as fuck to make your dreams a reality. And that is what I want to talk about in this chapter. So brace yourself for some bitter truths. Which hopefully will help you get outta the rut and into the A-game.

I hope I have made it clear by now that if you want to make positive changes in your business or life, it's going to take effort, and it's going to take work.

In a nutshell, anything that you want – and don't already have – is going to take discipline.

Nothing is easy.

Nothing happens overnight.

Getting good at your shit takes time.

Building an epic network takes time.

Growing a business takes time.

In fact, anything awesome takes a combination of time, effort and discipline. Fuck it, I'm going to invent a cool little formula:

Time invested + effort expended + disciplined behaviours = success (eventually).

Wow, that's not what you're usually fed by books like this, is it? Unfortunately, that's what works for the majority of folks. Not some sexy button-press formula.

Sorry. (Of course, if you're a freakish genius, crazy talented or can do stuff that we mere mortals can't do, then the whole experience can be far simpler.)

I want you to consider right now what you really want. How far do you want to take this? What does success actually look like for you, and how much time, effort and discipline are you willing to invest to make it happen?

I want to stress that there is nothing wrong with wanting a simple life or working a steady job. Absolutely nothing at all. In fact, it pisses me off when I see people slagging of others who have done that like they are fucking idiots for not going for it. If you are calling people like that idiots, you are calling my mum and dad idiots. Therefore, I want to slap you.

You can call those people idiots, though, if they complain and moan about their job every day. 'Cause then they need to change and choose the path that makes them happy. Lol.

I digress.

Not everyone should go for it. Launching a business, chasing your dreams, quitting your job and going 'Fuck it, I'm going to do my own thing' is *not* right for everyone. Some people either don't have what it takes to make it or don't truly comprehend how much time, effort and discipline it actually takes.

Anyone who is pitching you the concept of having it all, right away at least, is selling bullshit disguised as chocolate. I've fallen for that crap myself, and I see people falling for it time and time again.

Yes, in time you *can* have it all. But, as I have said quite a few times now, not only does it involve effort and discipline, it also involves a degree of sacrifice. You have to be comfortable with cutting back, letting go or losing something for a period of time at the start of your journey to get what you want.

There are only so many hours in a day, there is only one of you, and you can only be stretched so thinly if you want to go all in.

Let me explain what I mean about going all in.

I was offered an opportunity after what can only be described as the selection process from hell. Quite frankly, I was worked like a dog, and every single day I waited for an email to see if I'd made it to the next round. My fitness business had spanked me, I had no cash spare and I really needed this, I might add.

Anyway, I was presented with an opportunity – but that opportunity (although totally legit) would cost me the grand sum of $1,000.

I did not have $1,000.

If I converted my Great British Pounds, I think I had about $30 spare.

Now I had flirted with risk before, but although I had pushed the envelope, I had never really gone balls deep. The little voice in my head kept telling me this was a huge mistake; I was going to fail; I would end up in all kinds of trouble if I did it.

So – and this is *not* advice I recommend – what happened was I took the bottle of twenty-one-year-old whisky, a birthday present which I'd been saving for special.

I drank the whisky.

I took my AMEX (which I had applied for in case exactly this opportunity came up), and apparently – because I have no memory of this – silenced the annoying voice and paid the $1,000.

Waking up, I felt like death – and looked at the notification on my screen. It was an introduction. The gentleman – Ryan, whom I have spoken about previously – had had it planned all along. In fact, there had been two of us in the running for this opportunity.

I was the one who took the plunge.

He knew that I was poor as piss, so he had arranged for me to do work on his behalf that would cover the cost of the coaching. But I wasn't told this until after I had invested, and here we are now. Just taking that risk and deciding to go balls deep allowed me to get the best marketing, sales funnel, and business mentorship ever.

Plus Ryan (now a good friend of mine) opened me up to his network. Which in itself has been worth much more than I paid.

That incident gave birth to my legendary 'AMEX gamble'. Which is where I make a calculated risk, invest, have no idea how I'm going to get the money and simply make it happen!

Of course, it could have gone completely nipples north, but it didn't. And if it did? Well, I have learned to embrace failure. Not in that stiff upper lip way, pretending I don't care but really wanting to have a little cry. But in the way that, if I fail at something, I have simply given myself an opportunity to learn and do better next time.

History is littered with examples of people who have failed over and over again but didn't give up. These folks became people who have changed the world. Yes, they were stubborn, probably didn't listen to advice and were no doubt told to quit time and time again. The difference is, instead of doing the same things, they learned, adapted, improved, and went for it again.

I love that shit!

A harsh reality is that, although you may think people are waiting for you to fail, laughing at you, saying things behind your back, most of the time they are too concerned with their own problems to be bothered with you and yours. That may be hard to take, but please do – because it's awesome!

Think about it for a moment. If you could try something new – let's say, launch a business that you have been itching to do and not a single person would know if you fucked up – would you?

I bet you would.

People are so worried about what other people think of them that they simply, time and again, do nothing. You need to get it into that noggin of yours that you are not on people's minds as much as you think.

So set your goal.

Be relentless.

Go for it.

To hell with what anyone says.

Show up every day. This one has been a recent epiphany for me, as it's only in the last year that I have done exactly that.

Rain or shine.

Happy as a clam or hating all of the peoples.

Every day – for my clients, in 'Coffee With Dan', my team – I show up. Whether I want to or not. I have made a commitment to my audience and clients, and I serve them whether I am in the mood (I usually am, btw) or not.

I'm going a little cheesy here, but think of the story of the tortoise and the hare. I'm not going to go over it again, but consistent, steady daily progression – over time – tends to yield success. The bands of yesteryear that are still massive now, spent years in shitty little vans, touring grotty pubs and playing to an audience of three who didn't want them there in the first place. Or were too drunk to notice. Bringing it up to date, there are multi-millionaires on YouTube, for example. Did they make their millions overnight? No. What they did was consistently put out content, over and over again, for years.

So yes, the people in both these examples, and all the other individuals who have time served in their craft, deserve their success. There was absolutely zero guarantee that they would ever make anything from their efforts, but they were consistent. They showed up every day.

Being relentless, again, is key here to getting the results you want. When you are starting out in whatever you are doing and you get no likes, no views, no comments, no enquiries, it can be utterly disheartening. The thing that will differentiate you from the others is whether or not you give up.

I've stressed before that you do need a degree of skill, and you have to have a product or service that people actually want (and enough of those people to serve). But if we say you do have all those things in place, or are at the very least aggressively working your way towards them, then being a relentless little shit and refusing to quit is the small difference that makes all the difference.

Channel your inner terrier and don't give up.

Be pleasantly annoying. This one is tricky to explain, and I'm going to be upfront and say that occasionally you will piss some people off. The good news is you can always get out of that, as I'll explain in a bit.

I'm going to go back to my headhunting days to illustrate this exactly.

147

My job was to make calls. Lots of calls, every single day, to try and find open vacancies that I could fill.

One huge company, one of the biggest employers of the candidates in my niche, was obviously a good target for my efforts. First time I called, I was hung up on.

I tried again a few days later.

This time I got 'We don't deal with people like you'.

So, I thought I would have fun with this. I set a reminder in my diary and, every Tuesday at 11am, I would call. I was always polite, always courteous. I would introduce myself and be promptly told to, 'Do one'.

Now I wasn't being an annoying little shit just for the sake of it. I had actually sourced some of the most highly skilled people for my database, and I knew this company had vacancies. The key thing here was that I knew they had a need, and I knew I could fulfil it. I had done my homework – and I suggest before you pleasantly annoy someone that you make sure you can actually help them or what you are offering is of value specifically to them.

Anyway. All I needed was one chance.

This went on for months. It went from them answering and hanging up to slightly longer conversations. Then the recruiting manager started joking with me that no matter how hard I tried, she would never work with me, and I joked back that I would never give up.

Over time, the conversations became longer and longer and we got to know one another. In fact, one Tuesday I missed the 11am call (I was sick as a dog) and *she* actually rang *me* asking where my call was!

Then came the day she had a position that she couldn't fill – and she stated to me that although this job had been on the books, no one had come close to filling it. This was my one and only shot.

I sent over one candidate.

A perfect fit.

They got the job.

As a result I became the only recruiter to serve this company, which made me alone around ten grand in commission, and multiple times that for my employer.

So, I hope you can see that being pleasantly relentless is very much a good thing.

And if you piss someone off? Just give them some space, spend a few quid on a gift of some description (don't be cheap), apologise for your actions – but explain why you did it (so make sure you had a good reason for chasing them in the first place) and leave it with them.

For me, anyway, they have come back every time. Works a charm.

Be varied. One thing you need to consider when you are being relentless in trying to pitch your idea, connect with someone or close some business is that everyone responds in different ways. I respond very well to one method of communication (and I'm not going to tell you, because if you want to get in touch – I want you to discover it for yourself).

Simply put, make a list of every possible communication method you can for the person or business you are looking to reach. From email to postal address to mobile number to social media to comments on their content to events to publications – make a big fat list. Then each week, try one.

Sounds so simple, doesn't it?

I've taught this to numerous people after my mentor taught it to me, but most people are simply too lazy to do it. All you need is a spreadsheet or notepad to keep track of everything, and each week commit to trying to reach them by a different medium. And when they respond? That's the medium they prefer.

So go do your thing.

Don't be attached to the outcome. This one has been a game-changer (sigh) for me. Doesn't need too much in the way of explanation, but it is really hard to do. Once you have mastered it, though, it can change your life.

Simply put, you want to be as emotionally unattached to the outcome of whatever it is you are doing as possible. Let me give you some examples.

Pitched an idea? Whether people like it or not – it doesn't matter.

Or to put it in a more intimate way, asked someone out? Whether they say yes or no – it doesn't matter.

If you can remove the emotion from the outcome, you will not only find yourself far less stressed but happier too. Getting too attached to a yes or no can drive you insane. When you let it go everything simply gets better.

That, and because humans are pretty fucked up, the less interest you show in the outcome emotionally, the more often things go your way.

Don't over-celebrate the wins. Don't commiserate the losses. They are just things. In the grand scheme of things, with your limited time here on the earth, they really don't matter.

You ain't dead.

You're still breathing.

Don't sweat it.

Move on.

Oh, and if in doubt, work harder. It's not forever...

Ha!

BE RELENTLESS TO DO/ACTION STEPS

Ask yourself right now what you really want. This sounds all woo-woo, but trust me – you need to have a vision of what you actually want. What is it going to look like, and just as important, are you willing to invest the time and energy to make it happen? By the way, it's totally OK if you don't, but you need to get clear on this!

Make sure you're showing up every single day. I say this all too often, but it's the truth. Show up. Every. Day. Make a commitment to your audience and the clients you serve – and by the way, it doesn't matter if you feel like it or not. Make sure you show up. The one thing that will differentiate you from the others is whether or not you give up.

Don't follow the herd of sheep. Be varied. Right now, make a list of every possible communication method you can think of for the person you are trying to reach. Don't be the person who only communicates on Facebook or via email. Don't be lazy. Grab yourself a notepad or spreadsheet to keep track of everything. Each week commit to trying to reach people you want to connect with using a different medium and note their response.

Stop attaching yourself to the outcome. Want to feel far less stressed? Get out of your own way and detach yourself from the outcome. You'll be happier too. Let go and everything will simply get better. Humans are pretty fucked up; the less interest you show in the outcome emotionally, the more often things go your way. Weird, right?

11

BE NICE

Be nice to people on your way up because
you might meet 'em on your way down.
ALEXANDRE DUMAS PERE

Look at that quote closely, because it harbours the essence of
this chapter in one sentence. Don't be a douche on your way
up the success ladder, because douches rarely stay at the top.
And when (if!) you come down, you'll have all those upset
people to deal with.

Often people forget the efforts of individuals who actually
helped them get to where they are. They become egotistical
and start to believe that they are a one-man band, which rarely
is the case – and this is why I have a whole bloody chapter
basically dedicated to thanking those who have been there for
me.

This chapter is all about not being a dick. And helping others
along the way, as well as acknowledging the people who have

helped you get where you are. Don't skip it, as it may just save your butt!

This chapter could easily be a one-pager.

In fact, it could be summed up in one line: 'Don't be a dick!'

Or you could phrase it as: 'You don't have to be a dick to succeed'.

Really. You don't.

Now, at points I may have come across as a bombastic, possibly arrogant, definitely vulgar crass arsehole. It's one of the tools I have at my disposal. I was like this at points because I myself have read all the books, watched all the trainings, been to all the events... and done nothing.

My goal was to get you either inspired enough or pissed off enough to take action. That's all I want for you.

So take the concepts, the ideas, the strategies and the tactics and just fucking do it. Whatever it may be – the thing that's been in your head for years that you have wanted to get out; the person you have put off speaking to; the risk you have never quite got round to taking – simply go for it.

Look, I am actually a nice guy. No, really! Although I seem to have this online persona, coupled with the fact that, in my current social media profiles, I am holding a chainsaw and laughing maniacally, I truly, genuinely care about people and want to help them as I have been helped.

Does that make me soft or a pussy? Well, that's your call to make. And, like any thought or feeling you have, it is completely your right to think whatever you want.

All I know is that I have, and have had for a long time, a burning desire to make sure my sister is cared for, repay my family for the sacrifices they made and provide a comfortable living for myself, my partner (pending) and mini Dans and Danettes (definitely pending). That, and I truly want to serve my audience to the best of my abilities. I want each and every interaction I have with my tribe to be positive, make an impact, inspire them or simply make them smile.

Does that sound like the motives of an arsehole?

No, it doesn't.

I'm fully aware that I'm *probably* limiting myself from billionaire status as, quite frankly, I don't have the personality or the energy to be a ruthless fuck. Not saying that billionaires (or multi-millionaires for that matter) *are* ruthless fucks, but from what I've read and observed so far, you do have to have a tough side.

For all my meatiness, lifting massive weights, boxing and glorious beard growth, I'm still the same Dan inside who cried as a kid at *Charlotte's Web*, used to save wild animals that had been hurt, put a cold flannel on my sister's head and sat with her when she had a fit.

I just don't have it in me to be a c*nt! Yep, saved the C-bomb for last, because it's true. I don't have that side, and I don't ever *want* to have that side. Sure, this might never yield me golden space yachts – but then again – it might. Safe to say I'm doing OK, right?

If you (like I am) are committed to leaving this planet better off than when you got here, who knows what you can achieve? The only limitation, really, is you.

This chapter is based on advice that I have picked up, and things I have fucked up, along the way.

Don't let others influence how you feel. This one is a biggie, and one of the hardest things to do. So it does take a lot of practice.

We have all had days when a shitty email, an irate phone call or something on social media makes our blood simply boil. As a result, it ends up ruining our day, and that negative interaction makes our interactions with other people shittier.

That's why I purposely don't check my email or social media inboxes until after I have put myself in a good mood.

You may have heard this before (as I have invested in some excellent mindset coaches), but there is a key tenet. That tenet is that thoughts are just that. You allow them to become feelings by the meaning you give to them. You allow them to become actions by how you react to those feelings. People who put negativity out have merely influenced you to do the one thing they probably wanted you to do in the first place – namely be pissed off.

By doing this, you are allowing people control over you. You don't want to do this, by the way. Remember earlier I said that you need to become detached from the outcome? This is one of the places you *really* need to do this.

At the end of the day, these annoyances are just words on a screen, voices in your ear or a bunch of pixels. Despite seeming real, they're not real. They aren't kicking down your door and smacking you around the face, are they? If you react how others want you to react, not only have they won, but you will likely do some dumb shit that you will no doubt regret.

And this leads neatly on to my next point, and what to do about it.

Be mindful of what others may be going through. So you got a shitty message asking for money. Someone complained and wasn't happy with the quality of your work. Perhaps you got told never to speak to someone again after you called them.

I know, I've been there. This happens. Not often, but it does happen. And when it does, especially if you are totally taken off guard, it can make you feel like a pile of shit.

But I want you to consider before you act what *the other* person could have been going through.

They could have just had a health scare, lost a loved one, have a sick child or any manner of things that life throws at us, and they are acting out of character, lashing out, as many of us do from time to time.

They could have had an argument with a spouse, business partner or colleague that has put them in a foul mood, and you were the next one up and got both barrels of their abuse.

Maybe they have been let down with a payment from a client at their end, and as a result they are trying to claw back cash even though you have done a great job. I've heard this one before: someone invested in your coaching, training, or educational material, didn't do the work, didn't make any difference to their life, and then realised they had no cash. They are now beating on your door trying to lay the blame on you so as to get a refund, even though it's their fault they failed.

These situations are many and varied, and it would take me quite some time to detail them all. However, when I'm faced with something like this, I have a solution that, for me anyway, works every time.

First, I write the most aggressive, venom-fuelled, 'fuck you' reply I can muster. I stick on some Prodigy or Metallica and smash the keyboard with all my creative rage. Then I take what I've written and save it in my notes.

I then carry on with my day and eventually go to bed.

The next day I read my reply. So far, I have never sent the pure rage that I had written. After going through the drill and getting a good night's sleep (and starting my day the right way), I find my responses are far more calm and collected, and I have generally come up with a solution of some description. If the other person continues to take it out on me, I have the upper hand as they have lost their cool and often make a knob out of themselves.

That's a win, I would say!

Never forget where you come from. I've already told you plenty about my background, so I'm not going to dig up all that bollocks again. But one thing I am very mindful of is that I came, personally, from modest beginnings, and I can be returned in an instant to that state.

I've seen it happen to people before. Some people forget where they come from and become egotistical lunatics. Pulling their noses up at people who are at the stages they were at a few years ago. But then they lose everything.

Don't be that guy (or gal).

I find being mindful of my modest beginnings serves two purposes – as it is a state that I don't want to go back to, it motivates me to keep going when I am tired, grumpy or simply don't want to. Every time I stop, I increase my chances of going back to zero. It simply is the fuel to keep my fire going.

Secondly, when you've had nothing – I mean going bin-fishing for sandwiches after the shops close for the day, no idea how you're going to pay your bills, oh-fuck-oh-fuck-oh-fuck kinda nothing – it encourages you to make a few provisions when you can.

Clear your debt, or at least manage it. Try and borrow nothing, and always have some cash at your disposal. If you have debt, really focus (and yes, you may have to make some short-term sacrifices, but that's life) on paying it down.

I would advise you get your credit score as good as you can, and have a few empty credit cards on hand just in case you need to do an AMEX gamble of your own or are in a bind and need help with cash flow to tide you over. Do *not* rely on them.

This next one is a tough one but I would strive to do this.

Take 30% of what you earn, put it aside as tax. Don't fuck with the taxman. Just put it aside and don't touch it. One year I didn't do this and nearly killed myself with the amount of work I did to make sure I made the payment.

To save or not to save? That is a big question. I think it is totally dependent on you as a person. For example, I haven't previously saved, although now I have accumulated some robust funds from doing business because when my account was at zero or in the red, it forced me to take action and get shit done.

For you, it may be very different. If you have a family or dependents then I would suggest having at least three months, six if you can, of liveable wage saved. Totally your call.

Look after those who looked after you. A lot of people when they start to get successful forget the folks who helped them get to where they are. This is especially the case if you start to eclipse them. Now, a couple of folks have fallen out with me as I have grown – in their eyes – so very fast and surpassed where they are. However, I make a very clear reference to them and the assistance/coaching/contacts they gave me to help me get where I am in my life.

As you will see, I have a large 'Thank you' section at the end of this book, and have, to the best of my abilities, given thanks to everyone who has supported me on my journey. And I actually mean it. Without the combined effort and advice of all of them, I would not be where I am today.

It's not just those in the business world; each and every person who has been in my life and touched me in some way deserves credit for my success. It's not only fair, it's the right thing to do. Make sure you do the same. It goes a long way, and you never know when you will need to lean on them again.

Don't burn your bridges.

My philosophy. This is a culmination of a few of the key points I touched on earlier.

I have been blessed to have had help, advice, coaching, mentoring and support from some of the best in the world. As I've already said, I wouldn't be here if it wasn't for them.

I have a responsibility, nay a duty, to fulfil. The first part is to help myself. I have to secure my own health, skills, finances and business first.

The next part of my duty is to help others achieve what *I* have (to whatever degree they wish to, in whatever area they need), and help them get to my level.

Then, it is my duty to help others, give back, and support those who need it.

Once I have done this?

I simply wash, rinse, repeat and plough on to the next level – whatever the fuck that ends up being!

I am fortunate enough to have a lot of energy that I can spare, and I am more than happy to make the investments, put in the time and do the work to get shit done. I do it so others don't have to.

And I'm cool with it. Like I said, I live to serve. It may sound a little self-sacrificing, but I don't see it that way. I enjoy it. I like helping people; it makes *me* feel good, so I selfishly indulge in it.

I like feeling good.

How can I make an impact in this world if I am stingy and keep all the secrets (lol – I still see that crap all the time) to myself? That doesn't make me a good person.

It makes me a dick.

And, as I said way back at the beginning of this chapter, if you take away just one thing from this – simply don't be a dick!

BE NICE TO DO/ACTION STEPS

How to stop your blood boiling. Don't. Check. Your. Emails. First. Thing. In. The. Morning! Put yourself in a good mood before you jump into the bullshit hurricane of emails, social media and messages. Once you're in a good mood, you'll find you won't be running your day with negative interactions.

Be mindful of what others are going through. Consider before you act how the other person might be feeling and what they may have gone through. If you get a shitty email or bad message, do this: first write the most aggressive, venom-fuelled, 'fuck you' reply you can think of. Take what you've written and pop it in your notes. Carry on your day as normal and forget the message. The next day, reread the pure rage you have written. You'll find the next time you look at the aggressive message, your response will be much calmer and more collected.

Look after those who have looked after you. This one pretty much speaks for itself. Don't burn your bridges. The first part is to help yourself. You have to secure your own health, skills, finances and business first. Once that's all in check, the next part of your duty is to help others.

THE END

Well, that was quite a ride, wasn't it?

We're finally at the end of a somewhat brutal, hopefully entertaining, maybe a little offensive but, if I have done my job right, useful journey.

Look. One thing I hope I have made clear is that I am not special. Neither are you. We're just humans with similar wants, needs and desires. But what we all are is unique.

Whatever DNA soup your parents concocted made you.

That's the difference between you and me.

There are things that, quite frankly, I can kick your arse on. Equally, there will be things that you can make me look a bloody toddler at.

The only difference right now (and if you are already doing this, you are a fucking hero) is the fact that I am doing. While you are thinking about doing.

I remember, back in my headhunting days, a guy telling me that he was an ideas man. That's what I used to identify with: I'm extremely creative and can come up with some seriously different solutions to problems.

Thing is, any fucker can have ideas. What I realised when I got older was that every Tom, Dick and Harry (or, er, Sarah, Vicky and Kylie, if you prefer) has ideas.

So. Bloody. What.

What counts is you taking that idea, and making it a reality.

And how do you do that?

By doing the fucking work!

The books you can find online that tell you to follow your passion, go for your dreams and live a life of freedom are many. In fact, I read a fair few of them when I first got the itch about four years ago.

Boy, did they inspire me to change my life!

Did I though?

Did I heck!

THE END

It was only when I went balls deep, all in, made the relevant sacrifices in my life, invested in my education, skills and network, put time in every single day, and never, ever quit that my life began to change. And the ball started rolling.

As entrepreneurs we are always growing, and even I'm not perfect. Far from it. I'm going through the same growing pains that all entrepreneurs and business owners go through as they try to scale, reach more people, and keep making a profit without becoming a scumbag. At times I have had:

- Cash flow issues
- Staff issues
- Health and fitness issues
- Sanity issues!

But I wouldn't change it for the world. I am finally doing the one thing that I truly believe I was put here to do – leading people by the hand, or kicking them up the arse, to get the shit they have been putting off forever done.

It's rather fun, if I'm honest. Ha!

But fun aside, I've realised that I have been gifted a group of people who loyally follow me, invest in me, share my highs and lows and never falter. It would make me a selfish prick if I only used this tribe of quite frankly terrible (but awesome) humans just to line my own pockets.

It would make me, in fact, a dick.

So as of now, I am still trying to figure out exactly who I am, what the point of me is, and what impact I can make. And I'm going to apply this directly to my audience. With time, I am going to use this tribe of fruitcakes to create massive changes in the entrepreneurial landscape.

As always, I don't know what I'm going to do, how I'm going to do it, or what it's going to look like, but I know it will happen. It will happen because I will do the work that is necessary to make it happen.

I'm a nature-loving, miniature-painting, film-obsessed bookworm who is rather fond of his own company. I am actually an introvert, would you believe? What you see now is years of discipline, working on myself, hard work and being a relentless little shit who refused to stay in his place. I am *not* the Dan I was fifteen years ago. Fuck, I'm not the Dan I was six months ago!

What I'm trying to say is that you – and the shite that's in your head, the stories that you are telling yourself – will be the only thing that holds you back from making the changes and going balls deep in what you truly want to do.

Don't let your mind fuck you over.

THE END

On paper, someone like me shouldn't really be doing what I am now. But I am. So in closing I want to say this:

Fuck the bullshit excuses that you give yourself.

Fuck the nonsense stories that you tell yourself over and over again.

Fuck the critics, the people who tell you it will never work or those who don't believe in you or your vision.

Fuck the people who say it's easy, doesn't involve hard work or effort.

Fuck staying in your place.

Fuck the status quo.

Fuck being average, full stop.

Learn to embrace life, love work, see failure as a friend, relish the act of creating something out of nothing but your own efforts, apply discipline to your life, buck the trend, swim against the stream, have a vision, have a dream, have a fucking reason so powerful you can't sleep at night.

And quite simply... BE AWESOME.

PERSONAL THANK YOUS

Personal thank yous to people who have helped me to get where I am, given me support and resources that I rate and whom I've learned from. (Please note – none of these people were consulted in the making of this book, so please don't hold anything against them. They didn't make me like this).

THE PEOPLE WHO HAVE BEEN IN MY NON-BUSINESS LIFE

Without you all I wouldn't be the (amazingly, and quite surprised still) successful fruitcake I am now:

Debra and Nigel Meredith – I have literally no idea how you put up with me! Your parenting, relationship and how you deal with life's blows have been an inspiration. Honestly, I couldn't ask for better parents – thank you.

Anna Meredith – ahhh, Spud. You are the source of so much inspiration, yet also a pain in the arse! I know life hasn't dealt you the best of hands, but your big brother loves you and will never, ever let you down.

Tobo, Chambers, Barnett, The Griffiths, The Collings, The Mighty Cake, Dave and Neil – we may not have time to hang out quite as much anymore, but you are top lads. Yes, I know I have never used that phrase before, but it's my book so I can do what I want!

Ben Hazeldine – never would I think a walk around a marina would be the highlight of my day. Thank you for your belief – and smacking some sense into me from time to time. Lucky to have you as one of my closest friends.

Fran Dunne – you were with me for the toughest years of my entrepreneurial journey. You kept me going, you kept me sane, and you made sacrifices that many wouldn't have done. I wish you every happiness, and I hope your adventures land you the sunny, happy (hair free!) life you deserve.

Judith Williams – you had belief in me, when virtually no one else did. You provided that crucial first investment that started the ball rolling. Wouldn't be doing this if it wasn't for your faith/insanity!

INNER CIRCLE WORK PEOPLE AND THOSE WHO HAVE GONE ABOVE AND BEYOND

Tega 'Teggles' Diegbe. Never had a right hand man before – that's what I've always been! I have never had anyone work so hard, be a shoulder, and personify loyalty and commitment. My chocolate brother, you are something else.

Sarah Louise Carter – trying to organise and manage me = a thankless task. As assistants go, I couldn't ask for more, you wonderful and extremely tolerant human.

Andy 'Mutant' Davis and Cameron 'F-rocker' Shean – you took my fitness facility and made it shine. You have kept me – and my business – healthy, and have not broken anything yet either!

Mike Neck for giving me a fitness home when I had none, and opening up your gym and world to me when my life took a reset. Thanks, you big armed bastard!

Mike Samuels – one of my first coaching clients, and now partner in all things copy. Your ability to show no emotion and balance out my manic ways is nothing short of heroic.

Sean Mysel – true friend, pain in the arse, and one of the smartest guys I know. You are a gifted human, amazing writer, and I'm proud to have had you with me on this rather daft journey

Anna Selby – what you can do with social media is genius, and quite frankly, if I don't see you on TV one day I will be stunned. Thanks for supporting my vision, and giving me a kick up the arse when I need it – which is apparently very often.

Emma Melhuish – my first business partner! Small thumbs, but a genius with online advertising and even better friend. Uncle Dan – I promise – will be a bad influence on your little one, ha!

Mark Whitehand – long haired, northern, daft-as-balls soft-lad who happens to be an amazing coach, even better videographer and genuine friend who goes the extra mile. Proud of you.

Ollie Matthews – my first ever coaching client and now very good friend. You took the plunge. Your positivity is infectious.

Nayar Pervez and Alex Holowko – you believed in what I do, and have been with me on this ride since the start. Your epic talents with words and inability to say no is glorious.

Franc Feliu for being my partner in the craziest journey I have taken yet, and for forcing my hand to write this bastard book.

Ryan Levesque – the man the AMEX gamble was made for and the first man to take a real chance on me. Honestly, without you – 100% – I wouldn't be here right now. Simple as that. I love you, man. End of. I will always have your back.

Ryan Lee for giving me my first proper shot at the stage in the entrepreneurial world. A supportive friend and someone I simply love to work with.

Ben Settle – even though you profess to be a tough S.O.B., I appreciate you giving me a shot – and for going the extra mile for a friend. What you have taught me is immense. That, and you like me, really…

Chris Burgess and Luke Johnson for giving me your audience in those early days when I was just starting out in copy.

Joe Gregory – *epic* levels of commitment to getting this book together, figuring out how to get the nonsense out of my head and into print.

Justin Devonshire, Stephen Somers, Jamie Alderton and Pat Divilly – couldn't ask for a better group of lads to be on this journey with. Bloody geniuses, the lot of you. Thanks for all you have done – and continue to do.

Dexter Abraham – a mentor and friend like no other, both inspiring and terrifying in equal measure. You helped make me the man I am today, showed me what was possible and toughened me up. Thank you for believing in me and being there in the dark times – I know it's been a thankless task at times, but I am more grateful than you can ever imagine.

THE EMOTIONAL SUPPORT NETWORK

Brian Grasso, Carrie Campbell, Shari Teigman, Rob Michon, Erik Rokeach, A J Mihrzad, Marci Lock, Dax Moy, Michael Lassen, Kirsten Roberts, The Wildes, Carly Jennings and Edi Tsang. Let's face it, I'm as loopy as a bucket of frogs on LSD. Appreciate you being the buffers to my bowling lane of sanity.

Also – bloody hell, that's a lot of you! Poor bastards!

THE COACHES AND MASTERMINDS WHO ARE, QUITE FRANKLY, THE TITS

John McIntyre – you made Titans weird, but without your introductions I would be buggered.

Derek Johanson for creating Copy Hour, showing me the ways of words and generally tolerating me during those early days.

Rob Hanly – my first ever coaching call! You are the epitome of class when it comes to coaches. Epic human all round. Also epic beard.

John Logar – my first ever coach! I don't think I have met anyone who has over-delivered like you. You took some coal and made a rough-as-balls diamond, ha!

Doberman Dan Gallapoo – I had no idea why you took me under your wing in those early days. Still don't now! Appreciate you, and your wife, ha!

Paul Mort and Tim Goodwin – you gave me my first taste of this world, and both deserve success in your ventures. Fact.

Tina Marie for giving me a shot at the big leagues and sorting out my utter lack of organisation in the early days. You have skills, woman. Massive thumbs up to Darren Casey for recommending you in the first place.

Jonathan Rivera for pushing me to podcast and being an epic co-host and producer. I do enjoy our chats.

Michael Lovitch and Hollis Carter for asking me to join the Baby Bathwater Institute *and* allowing me back. Amazing – the highlight of my year.

Brian Kurtz and Michael Fishman – you gave a newbie sage advice, and I have never forgotten 'Don't look down!'

Brian Noonon, Mike Gelblicht and Morgan Crozier – skilled coaches, reliable colleagues and friends. Solid and smart humans.

Joe Polish – the connections and friends I have made through GENIUS network have been invaluable. I'll never quite forget that Halloween party, though…

Andy Hussong and Todd Brown – seriously smart mofos and utterly generous with their time and genius. I hope to be as skilled as you when I grow up.

Andre Chaperon – a truly gifted writer, but I'll never forget *that* book you gave me. Changed it all for me, buddy.

IN CLOSING

To everyone who invested in me when I was fresh.

THE END

To the early adopters when I launched CLUB5.

To the truly brave and wonderful folks who came with me for a year in PLATINUM.

To the special folks who want more Dan in 'Espresso With Dan'.

To the peeps who have joined and continue to pour into 'Coffee With Dan' every day.

To everyone who has lent their genius to my group for free to share their amazing talents.

To everyone I have met on this crazy journey. (And this sounds like such a dick move, but there are too many of you to reference!).

And finally, to each and every person who has *ever* invested in me, whether with your money, your time or simply by following me and supporting me on a journey that will end I have absolutely no fucking idea how.

Thank you.

Thank you.

Thank you.

BOOKS AND COURSES TO GET HOLD OF

Yo.

I have referenced the amazing books and courses I have used in this book, as well as people you should follow. First of all, I would Google some of those folks – trust me on this, OK?

Secondly, I have *so* many damn books and courses and folks I'd happily recommend (no affiliate or commission crap – I recommend them because I have used them). If you get my business tips – www.coffeewithdan.com/118things – I'll make sure to include a resources section at the back. That cool? There are too many to list here, and quite frankly, in the writing of this book I think I have forgotten how to use my brain!

ABOUT THE AUTHOR

Hello. My name is Dan Meredith. I'm a plum.

I have somehow gone from worker bee and vaguely decent success across a variety of industries, including fitness, advertising and copywriting, to having a tribe of over 4,000 (probably more by the time you read this) entrepreneurs worldwide, hundreds of clients all over the world, a copywriting business, a gym, a stack of digital courses, a marketing agency…

And now a book!

You are holding it, by the way.

Throw in the fact that I count some of the most successful marketers, business people and pioneers as friends, and it really is rather silly.

Just a few years ago my choice was between petrol in the car and eating. Now, as long as I have my iPhone and Internet connection, I'm good to go anywhere in the world.

Pretty cool, eh?

But no matter how successful I get, how many places I speak at, how many people I help, I will still look like a fucking badly shaved bear. Swings and roundabouts.

You can get hold of me, join my crazy tribe and take part in the silliness too at www.coffeewithdan.com.

MY GIFT TO YOU

The fucking awesome cheat sheet – 118 tactics that can skyrocket your success. Like really – you know, 3, 2, 1 countdown, fire and spaceship, the full works!

I hope you have enjoyed this book. It's been in my head for quite some time, and as I said waaaaaaay back in the beginning, if you get just one thing from it, it's done its job.

And I'll be a happy plum.

But I know that I've read books before and got myself all fired up only to think, right, now what the fuck do I do?

I don't want that to happen with this book. As it's all about getting shit done. Not leaving you stranded when the tyres hit the road.

So to prepare this bad boy cheat sheet for you, I went full geek and devoured my 'Daily Dose Of Dan' posts in 'Coffee With Dan', all my trainings and webinars, and whipped out 118 of my best tips across a variety of subjects, including sales, marketing, product development, copywriting, mindset, networking, social media, advertising and tribe building (as well as quite a few more topics). And some great titbits from the awesome experts I have dragged into my world too.

This cheat sheet alone has cost me tens, if not hundreds (I lose count and keep going to more things), of thousands in courses and is the best of what I know, right now.

Depending on when you are reading this, the cheat sheet may be different. I'm not so arrogant as to think I know everything, because that would be complete horse shit. As I learn more stuff, I'll update the sheet.

So, if you want to grab the best of what's in my brain, simply head over to www.coffeewithdan.com/118things and I'll send it to you right away.

It will be formatted so, if you want to, like me you can print it off, and it will look the tits as well. Might it be worth doing that? You can then keep it with you and highlight the tactics as something to do in your business. Or you might want to sit in your underwear and watch Netflix eating pizza.

Both are fucking awesome!

And, did I mention, I fuckin' love pizza?